ATHEISTIC HUMANISM
and
THE BIBLICAL GOD

ATHEISTIC HUMANISM
and
THE BIBLICAL GOD

José Maria Gonzalez Ruiz

TRANSLATION BY

AMADO JOSÉ SANDOVAL, S.J.

THE BRUCE PUBLISHING COMPANY / *Milwaukee*

Nihil obstat: Richard J. Sklba, S.S.L., S.T.D.
                Censor librorum

Imprimatur: ✠ William E. Cousins
              Archbishop of Milwaukee

              December 16, 1968

The *Nihil obstat* and *Imprimatur* are a declaration that a book or pamphlet
is considered to be free from doctrinal or moral error. It is not implied that
those who have granted the *Nihil obstat* and *Imprimatur* agree with the
contents, opinions, or statements expressed.

Library of Congress Catalog Card Number: 69-18134

Copyright © 1969 The Bruce Publishing Company
Made in the United States of America

FOREWORD

When the Church, gathered in council, attempted to discern and define her relationship with "the world today" (in the famous schema XIII), many Christians looked upon this as a bit of apostolic opportunism designed to make an immutable truth fit changing conditions—certainly a legitimate task, but one which is rather superficial in the long run, and not too attractive.

The problem itself goes far beyond such an *aggiornamento*, and this is what Vatican II has done in giving form to the inspiration of John XXIII. If it is true that the very *being* of the Church has reference to the world (it is the earthly site of her incarnation in grace), it is reasonable to assume that the Church will respond then—in this search for the world and in her open dialogue with it—to the radical demands of her early inspiration. This means that in order to have an authentic understanding of her task, we must go beyond mere sociological surveys (even though they are quite pressing) of man's new condition in a scientific and technological civilization. (Cfr. the Introduction to the Pastoral Constitution promulgated at the end of the Council.) It is to the Gospel that we must go, to the original "Good News" itself. Once again the dialectical principle comes into effect according to which the presence of the Church in the world becomes precisely the starting point for the *return to the Gospel*. This the Council itself recognized explicitly.

Therefore, our faith is filled with enlightening joy when we see a Scripture Scholar teaching us how to read in scripture the laws of commitment of the Church to history, and presenting us with a "theology of the world."

But this task does not reach only to the four gospels, despite their undeniable preeminence. It is the whole testament of the new covenant, whose human, historical and cosmic dimensions are uncovered for us by Paul in the person of Christ who takes on a human body. And together with the New Testament and Christ, the whole Old Testament comes into our view of the economy of salvation and liberation. For here we deal with the God of Abraham, Isaac, and Jacob, not the God of the philosophers and deists. The whole law of Moses actually tends toward the evangelical law, in which the precepts are nothing but pedagogic dispositions to love. Every event in the history of Israel is a preparation for and a fore-shadowing of what will happen to the "people of God." All the prophetic announcements of the Messiah in a kingdom of justice and liberation are now coming into effect. These prophecies are being realized as they become operative through their eschatological tendency.

The "people of God," moreover, definitely established by God's coming into history, is from then on the witness and main actor of the incarnation of divine life in Jesus, the God-man. The Messianic era, therefore, has begun. Its stages are imposed on the history of the world. This does not mean that the progress of earthly civilizations constitutes the Kingdom of God. It comes from above, and still is a totally gratuitous, loving act. But this love implies precisely an ontological and historical commitment to an evolving humanity—humanity, and not merely a juxtaposition of isolated individuals. It is only natural, then, for the people of God to recognize in Creation (whose main character it is) and in the series of human generations incorporated in Christ, that it constitutes the place where the divine life—"grace"—finds its rhythm and its laws, according to the development of an "economy" wanted by God.

At this point we are far from a conception of the "sacred" or of "religion," which embodies and gathers together the elements and values of the sacred. It is no longer a question of man receiving favors from an awesome and inaccessible divinity. The God of love becomes man, the brother of all men, and takes the initiative in a communion which is far from a mystic escape. If there is an aliena-tion, it is God who alienates himself, so to speak, becoming "someone else," emptying himself somehow of his divinity (St. Paul). The sacred manifestations—both necessary and positive—will undergo a transformation and will be re-clothed in faith in Christ's "sacraments." The word "supernatural" is stripped of its ambiguities, both religious and anthropological. Eschatology is an inner motion of history.

What fills us with joy and light in Dr. José M. González Ruiz's "theology of the world" is the fact that it is presented as a speculative and apologetic elaboration which starts from the advances of science. It is the expression of a deep reading of the Bible, the sacred history which is the supreme criterion of all history and a living source of its divine meaning.

On October 19, 1964, in the 105th General Session of the Council, when schema XIII was presented (by then in its second draft) the late Cardinal Meyer, Archbishop of Chicago, pointed out that the project, though successfully worked out and structured, still lacked a theology of the world. He then proceeded to sketch that theology. This book represents a deep and organic elaboration of those important conciliar directives, with all their consequences, especially in the direction of a dialogue with contemporary atheism.

Thus we are happy to see this collection of studies of Dr. González-Ruiz, many of which were influential in the Council itself for the preparation of the great text of the Pastoral Constitution on the Church.

M. D. CHENU

CONTENTS

Contents

PART I
THE GOD OF
ABRAHAM,
ISAAC AND
JOSEPH

CHAPTER 1

THE NEW FRONTIER OF THE SACRED

For Judaism no less than for pagan religions the sacred was something isolated, enclosed within a given space outside whose boundaries all else was profane or "common." The liturgy consisted in the priests' entering the sacred temple to bring out some sacred particles and with them to sprinkle the profane world thereby consecrating it up to a point. "Religion" was the "ghetto" of the sacred, and in order to join it the profane area—the world—had to be abandoned and one had to seek sanctuary in the "*sancta sanctorum*," the only place where God issued his oracles.

Christianity destroys completely the barricades which made "religion" a haven in the world. It embraces everything profane, worldly, and "common," and by so doing makes it sacred.

This "sacralization" of the profane which Christianity claims is not a juxtaposition or an imposition—a kind of superficial ablution sliding over the plastic cover of the world—but a deep penetration to the very core of the "common" being, to give it a final and "eschatological" meaning which achieves its fulfillment. Human endeavor certainly remains unfinished as a result of death (of individuals, of nations and civilizations, of humanity); "divine grace," introduced by Christianity, inserts itself into the deepest parts of the worldly and human being. It gives it a rhythm which moves it toward the fulfillment of the human project. According to Christianity, man need not abandon the world to go to God. God is found—God must be found—in the world, in the very core of its being. In this perspective many passages of the New Testament acquire deeper meaning.

Jn. 4:20–24: We have passed beyond the "temple of Jerusalem-temple of Garizim" alternative, since God is no longer enclosed in any given sacred place. God walks through human life, just "like any other man" (Phil. 2:7).

Mt. 25:31–46: The "good people" will not be those who persistently searched for God in the temples, but those who—even unknowingly—looked for him, and found him, among the hungry, the thirsty, the prisoners, and the naked.

Mk. 2:27–28: There are no longer any exclusively sacred times—solely appointed for the service of God. The "Sabbath"—sacred time—has been put at the disposal of man. An omission in serving man can no longer be justified by the need to devote oneself to divine worship. That is to say, no one can offer a religious or cultic duty as an excuse for neglecting a human service.

Mt. 27:51: The veil isolating the *Sancta Sanctorum* is rent at the moment of Christ's death. There is no longer a "ghetto" of the sacred.

The use of hieratic titles—either from Jewish or Hellenic tradition —is carefully avoided in the New Testament when designating the ministers of the "new religion." They are never called "priests," but "guardians" (*episkopoi*), "elders," "shepherds." Christ never takes on a hieratic position. The institution of the great Christian act of worship takes place in the midst of a dinner with absolute normality, in an evident climate of "demythologization." The early Christians followed the same "profane" style in their liturgy, "breaking the bread in their homes." The first Christian generations at least fulfilled the pressing exhortation of Jesus not to call those in charge of the community "fathers" or "doctors." And they had not forgotten yet that "the greatest among them had to be as a servant." This explains the presentation of the apostles in the Synoptic Gospels and in Acts with a realism that is at times humiliating (doubts, denials, misunderstandings, etc.). There was no "triumphalism."

Acts Ch. 10: There are no longer "profane" or impure objects. Everything is edible, that is, everything can be intrinsically sacralized. In his discourse Peter says: "But God has shown me that I should not call any man common or unclean." God had said to Peter:

"What God has cleansed you must not call common" (Acts 10:15). This is the new thing about the Incarnation: God is present in the deepest core of human and earthly reality in order to render it sacred from within. The resurrection of Christ is the sure confirmation of the divine project. It is not a mere adventurous excursion in the fashion of the Greek gods.

The sacred-profane tension, therefore, cannot be conditioned by the existence of two camps, one of which must attempt to destroy the other in order to survive. This is the concept of "christendom," a degradation of Christianity. The sacred is not dubbed-in on the profane. The sacred has no reason to produce its own values in order to compete with the world of the profane. The sacred has no longer a "sanctuary." The ministers of the sacred "have no place to rest their heads." Their home is the world. As Paul VI said in Bethlehem: "Christianity is not removed from the world. Our only concern is to proclaim our faith. We demand nothing but freedom to practice this religion, this new link established by Christ our Lord between men and God, and freedom to offer it to whoever will willingly accept it. There are no human values that Christ had not respected, ennobled, and redeemed. The mission of Christianity is a mission of friendship among the nations of the earth."

The attempts to absolutize myth which have taken place so frequently throughout the history of religions have played an essential role in that marking-off of a frontier between the sacred and the profane.

First of all, in a wider sense, myth can be taken as any penetration of the human by the divine. In a strict sense, however, it is only the identification of this action with intramundane and immanent actions which is mythical. This identification, in turn, can be done in two ways: (a) as conceived in essentialist categories (substance, accidents), as for instance, the identification of the Holy Spirit with a hidden force of nature; and (b) as actually recognizable in itself, as for instance, when the *theios aner*—Christ—is presented in "miraculous" events as a "transparency" of the transcendence. In these two cases, there is properly speaking myth because there is a likening of divine action to physical causalities.

Thus understood, no one can deny that myth can easily be found in the Bible, in both Old and New Testaments. There one speaks of a penetration of the divine into the human, and that penetration is conceived of in essentialist categories and described in images which attract our attention.

In this respect, the Bible offers nothing significantly different from other religious events of ancient times. In the primeval stages of our culture, writes Mircea Eliade, religion maintains "openness" to a superhuman world—the world of the axiological values. These are "transcendent" insofar as they are revealed by divine beings or mythical ancestors. They become, therefore, absolute values, and a pattern for all human activities. These models are channeled through myths, whose purpose is primarily to awaken and maintain a consciousness of another world, of a beyond, of a divine world, or a world of the ancestors. This "other world" represents a superhuman, "transcendent" level of *absolute realities*. Myth is not in itself a guarantee of "goodness" or of morality. Its function is to reveal models and thus provide the world and human existence with meaning. So its role in the constitution of man is immense. Thanks to myth the concepts of *reality, value,* and *transcendence* begin to take shape slowly. Thanks to myth the world is observed as a perfectly articulated cosmos, intelligible and significative. By telling us how things were made, they also reveal by whom and why they have been made and in what circumstances. All these "revelations" concern man more or less directly because they form a "sacred history."[1]

To achieve a better understanding of the problem as presented by Bultmann,[2] we must start off precisely at this point. Myth is an attempt to be open toward the transcendent and is a description of a decisive action of the transcendent in human and earthly life. The psychological reason that compelled Bultmann to undertake his task of demythologizing the Bible is undoubtedly apologetic: modern man cannot accept the cosmic-spatial and narrative potpourri in which the salvation message of the Bible is served. In fact biblical myth speaks of "the power or powers that man thinks he experiences as foundation and limit of his world and of his task. Myth does it in such a way that through imagery those powers are brought down

[1]Mircea Eliade, *Aspects du mythe*, Gallimard, 1963, pp. 171–177 and ff.
[2]Mainly in his *"manifesto"* of 1941, *Neues Testament und Mythologie* in *Beiträge zur evangelischen Theologie*, vol. 7, Munich, 1941, reproduced in *Kerygma und Mythos*, ed. by H. W. Bartsch, 3rd. ed, 1954, pp. 19–48.

to the realm of the known world and of earthly forces, to the level occupied by humanity with its feelings, motives and possibilities. The beyond is represented as 'the here and now.' For example, the transcendence of God is expressed in terms of distance in space."[3]

A mythical exposition is given of the redemptive event itself not only in the Old Testament, but in the New Testament as well. In recent years the problem of demythologization achieved almost planetary proportions with the publication in March, 1963, of the book *Honest to God* by the Anglican Bishop of Woolwich, John A. T. Robinson. Within a year it sold a half million copies in the original English, not counting translations into other languages.

Robinson's starting point has the same apologetic motivation that urged Bultmann to his radical proposal of demythologization: the modern world cannot accept the supernaturalistic cosmic vision in which the biblical message concerning God comes wrapped. According to this cosmic vision the world exists on three levels, with God residing on the top level, from where he handles the threads of human and worldly affairs.

Robinson, however, does not accept the Bultmannian presentation of demythologization offhand. He offers three main objections.

(a) Bultmann has not overcome the scientific dogmatism of the previous generation when he affirms that no modern man can accept the biblical cosmology, because it conflicts with a vision tenaciously conceived of as definitive.

(b) His critique of mythology has nothing to do with his excessive historical-critical scepticism regarding the biblical narratives, especially those of the gospels, as for instance, his absolute denial of the "empty tomb."

(c) His intimate association with a particular philosophy (heideggerian existentialism) as a substitute for the mythological cosmic vision is historically and geographically conditioned.

In order to judge Robinson's position we have to keep in mind that his prime motivation is apologetic and pastoral. The whole problematic of the bishop of Woolwich is pervaded by English pragmatism. He acknowledges it at the end of his book: "To demythologize—as Bultmann would readily concede—is not to suppose that we can dispense with all myth or symbol. It is to stop depending on one particular mythology—the one that Tillich

---

[3]R. Bultmann, *op. cit.*, p. 22.

calls the 'superworld of divine objects'—which is in peril of becoming a source of incredulity, rather than an aid to faith. Any alternative language—for instance, of profundity—is bound to be equally symbolic. But it may speak more profoundly to the soul of modern man."[4]

We simply try to recognize the reality of myth in the Bible as a means of expression for transcendent truth, but keeping in mind that the cosmic vision that envelops these truths has only a relative value. In this sense demythologization is a constant attitude for the believer in order to keep his faith from becoming *idolatric*, in Tillich's felicitous expression.[5]

Nevertheless Robinson believes that demythologization does not have to reach that absolute minimum proposed by Bultmann which reduces the object of faith solely to the salvific action of God in Christ. In this respect Robinson is not very explicit, but from his writings it can be concluded that for him God's salvific action is contained in the *kerygma* with a certain richness of detail which remains valid even after the most rigorous demythologization. So, as opposed to the radical "deworldification" proclaimed by Bultmann, Robinson thinks he finds in the *kerygma* a message of absolute "worldification" of the sacred and of the divine: "The beyond, in the midst of our life, the holy in the common."[6] God and the world are not placed in an alternative relationship (either God or the world) but in a dialectical one (God in the world). In order to go to God man does not have to leave the world. God, so to speak, has taken flesh in our neighbor and in the universe. When Robinson speaks of an a-religious Christianity, he only wants to point out the suppression of this alternative. Perhaps a superficial reading of the book has been the cause of such bitter criticism, criticisms which moreover had no bearing on the problem presented by the bishop of Woolwich.

The problematic raised by Bultmann had a resounding echo also in Catholic theology, and only two years after his famous manifesto Pope Pius XII published an encyclical, *Divino Afflante Spiritu* (September 30, 1943), in which the problem of biblical demythologization was taken up lucidly and courageously.

---

[4]From *Honest to God*, by John T. A. Robinson. Pub. in the U.S.A. by the Westminster Press, 1963. © SCM Press Ltd., 1963. Used by permission.
[5]P. Tillich, *Dynamics of Faith*, Harper, New York, 1958, p. 109 ff.
[6]J. A. T. Robinson, *op. cit.*, p. 86.

The first assertion of the encyclical deals with the acknowledgement that certain forms of expression have a relative value, so that the force and extent of the meaning can be known only *a posteriori*, that is, by investigating the literary customs of the times. "What these forms of expression were the exegete cannot determine *a priori*, but only from a careful study of ancient oriental literature."[7] In other words, the problem of demythologization is urgent and the Catholic reader of holy scripture cannot avoid it.

The issue raised for Catholics differs radically from all the non-catholic demythologizing positions, for the basic reason that the Church possesses a guiding ecclesial authority which directs the whole process of demythologization.

For a Catholic the Bible can be validly read and interpreted only *in medio ecclesiae*. However, this ecclesial enthronement of the Bible does not imply the possession of a magic key to interpretation. Just the opposite. The ecclesiastical *magisterium* recognizes the necessity of dependence on scientific investigation, and Pius XII even affirmed courageously the inadequacy of the scientific exegesis of the first nineteen centuries of the Church. "But our own times too, we have the right to hope, can make their contribution to the more profound and accurate interpretation of Holy Scripture. There are many matters, especially historical, which were insufficiently or hardly at all developed by the commentators of past centuries, because they lacked nearly all the information needed to elucidate them."[8]

But the difference in the problem which demythologization creates for the Catholic and for the Protestant stands out most clearly on the issue of tradition, the *magisterium* and dogma. All through the centuries the Catholic Church has been building up a dogmatic formulation of the unique message received from Christ and the apostles. Oscar Cullmann goes so far as to admit a Bible, but only during the first apostolic generation. These are the confessions of faith.[9]

[7]*Divino Afflante Spiritu, Selected Letters and Addresses of Pius XII,* Catholic Truth Society, London, 1949, p. 134.
[8]*Divino Afflante Spiritu, op. cit.,* p. 132.
[9]O. Cullmann, *Les Premieres confessions de foi chrétienne,* Paris, 1943; *La Tradition: probleme exégétique, historique et theologique,* Neuchâtel-Paris, 1953.

However, this same dogmatic formulation of the ecclesiastical *magisterium* does not escape from a certain control of demythologization.

Shortly after the appearance of *Divino Afflante Spiritu* Fr. Henry de Bouillard brought up the problem of the relations between "experience" and "concept," distinguishing in the theological and conceptual knowledge between "affirmation" and "representation." The affirmation remains immutable, whereas the representation is evolutional and replaceable.[10] This position provoked a lively reaction among some Catholic theologians (Labourdette, Nicolas) who saw in the distinction a latent agnosticism, and affirmed that even the theological *terminology*, despite its greater elasticity, tends to be immutable and that the dogmatic formulations as such are final. Against this theological immobility arose C. Sträter and a group of Dutch theologians. According to them "the *reinterpretation of dogma* can have an orthodox meaning, but it can also be a deviation. If we mean by this that the dogmas must be stripped of their old clothing when it becomes already old fashioned—for instance, the ascension of Christ interpreted according to Ptolemy's system— then this reinterpretation has a perfectly Catholic sense. A truth can be translated by representations which are false in themselves but which in a given stage of civilization are accurate representations of the content. What was once really promulgated as dogma can never be dismissed, but it can perfectly well be integrated into more recent ideas, in which, through a relative change of perspective, it will go on living. At any rate, it is clear that reinterpretation of dogma acquires a meaning foreign to Catholicism when it is considered possible and necessary for the reason that our knowledge can never have more than a symbolic and pragmatic value."[11]

As we can see, Christian theology cannot escape the pressing problem of demythologization. Dividing the whole of Christian occidental theology into two large groups—perhaps in a too simplistic manner—namely, protestant and Catholic, we should be able to discover in each an infra-structural position which subconsciously determines the motions of the theological pendulum.

[10]H. de Bouillard, *Conversion et grâce chez St. Thomas d'Aquin*, Paris, 1944, pp. 211–224.

[11]C. Sträter, cited in *Informationes Catholiques Internationales*, 181 (1962), p. 31.

The Catholic "temptation"

The Catholic group—basically latin and quasi-mediterranean—has inherited from Greece and Rome its undeniable affinity for myth. The Greco-Roman intellectuals of classical times were deeply convinced of the anthropomorphic relativity of classical myth. Xenophanes, born ca. 565 B.C., did not hesitate to attack openly the Homeric *pantheon*: "There is a god above all gods, and all men; neither his form nor his thought has anything in common with mortal beings."[12]

And an author as deeply religious as Pindar rejects the "incredible myths."[13] The conception of God in Euripides is totally influenced by the criticism of Xenophanes. At the time of Thucydides the adjective *mythodes* meant "like a fairy tale and without evidence."[14] When Plato[15] criticises the poets for the way they picture the gods, he is probably addressing an audience already convinced beforehand.

Greek and Roman myths nevertheless survived all the processes of demythologization, and this despite the triumph of Christianity. The basic "rediscovery" achieved by the Renaissance was its restoration of pure and "classical" forms.[16]

In all honesty, we must admit that there is some hypocrisy in this position or at least some implicitly conscious schizophrenia. Myths are beautiful and comforting. They have also helped to hold together the great political-social structures which maintained the unity of the mediterranean world under the Roman Empire, throughout the period of medieval Christianity, and right up to the great colonial undertakings of modern times. The mediterranean world loves an expression insofar as it is precise and concrete. It feels a great temptation to tame the transcendent and to reduce it to clear, concise forms. Scholastic theology itself reached its peak in the mediterranean luminosity of the great Neapolitan, Thomas Aquinas.

All this explains the resistance of Catholic theology to the

[12]B., 23.
[13]Pindar, *I Olymp.*, 28 ff.
[14]Thucydides, *History*, I, 21.
[15]Plato, *Republic*.
[16]Cfr. J. Seznec, *The Survival of the Pagan Gods. The Mythological Tradition and its Place in Renaissance Humanism and Art*, New York, 1953, p. 320.

painful and risky problem of demythologization. Like the three disciples on Mt. Tabor it savors the precise luminosity of the external form. It seeks to settle in it for good, anticipating the kingdom of God which is an authentic *eschaton*. Only when the cloud disappears and the light of the vision has faded does it face the hard reality of the naked presence of a totally demythologized Christ.

The Protestant "temptation"

The Protestant world, on the contrary, anchored in the Lutheran *sola fides sola gratia*, undertakes a sincere and loyal battle against myth. The problem of mythologization must be removed once and for all. For that reason the reality of God's salvific action is reduced to a bare minimum and all that luminous spectrum of oriental literature is declared a mere form of expression. We cannot but recognize the religious grandeur of this search stripped of a totally transcendent God, who is completely "other" (*ganz anderer*), and whom we reach in a bold leap, with eyes blindfolded before a light about which we know absolutely nothing.

Dialectical tension: demythologization and remythologization

Which of the two extremes is the right one? Conforming mythologization or radical demythologization? M. E. Dahl, with the mediating sense of anglican pragmatism, suggests an "intermediate" solution which puts the tremendous problem of demythologization in the right track. "The only way in which such eschatological realities can be described is in the language of myth and parable. Consequently what is needed today is not de-mythologization but remythologization. No doubt in every age we must try to think systematically about myth and analyze the parable with imagination and discipline but neither must ever be 'liberalized.' This can lead to a false dogmatism and raises difficulties. It is a mystery we are dealing with, part of the secret counsels of God, and it must remain so until we see 'face to face.' "[17]

Perhaps this magnificent encounter in love of all the historical "christianities," which we are all witnessing today, will provoke a mutual enrichment, and we will learn not to settle down permanently in the luminosity of the cloud of Mt. Tabor or in the desert solitude of a theology without God.

[17]M. E. Dahl, *The Resurrection of the Body*, London, 1962, p. 95.

Our search must be continuous. Our faith does not free us from the constant task of dialectic demythologization and remythologization. Every attempt to avoid this dialectic tension—either to the right, settling down in myth; or to the left, eliminating it once and for all—is a great bourgeois sin against the itinerant and evolutionary dimension of one faith and one hope which moves toward an *eschaton* on the very frontier of history.

CHAPTER 2

THE BIBLICAL GOD IS GRATUITOUS

In the most striking forms of contemporary thought we frequently encounter a humanism which claims to be atheistic on the ground that it believes that man's "Promethean" vocation is incompatible with his acknowledgment of God as a superior being. Later on we will present in detail the various historical forms of this "humanistic atheism," especially as expressed in the marxist critique of religious alienation.

A profound reading of the Bible led Paul Ricoeur to formulate this bold statement: "Unlike Greek wisdom Christianity does not condemn Prometheus: according to the Greeks, the 'sin' of Prometheus lies in having stolen fire, the fire of arts and crafts, the fire of knowledge and consciousness. The 'sin' of Adam, however, was not the same. Adam's disobedience was not in being a technical and knowing man, but in having broken the vital bond with the divine in his experience as man. Thus the first expression of that sin is the crime of Cain, the sin against his brother, not a sin against nature; the sin against love, not the sin against existence as an animal without history."[1]

The restoration of Prometheus to the Christian calendar can only take place after a serious reflection on the God of the Bible.

The God of the Bible is not an immanent explanation of the human enigma

The first thing we must stress is the fact that the biblical God is not presented as an immanent solution to the human and cosmic enigma.

[1] P. Ricoeur, *History and Truth*, Northwestern University Press, Evanston, 1965, p. 85.

The scientific atheism of the century of the Enlightenment pretended to do without God because the God-hypothesis was no longer necessary to explain the riddle of life.

Throughout the Bible, on the contrary, God is presented as an unexplainable luxury. The divine presence is cosmic and human evolution is totally gratuitous. It cannot be grasped except through an explicit self-revelation by God himself. The biblical God breaks into the evolving reality of man under the total and absolute form of "grace" and of the "gratuitous."

Paul explicitly affirms in the first two chapters of his letters to the Romans that in the Greco-Roman religious world the degradation of the gratuitous revelation of God had been brought about culpably in a theism manipulated by the interest of the ruling classes, "who by their wickedness suppress the truth." (Rom 1:18)

The name of God was sacred, and to speak it could accredit the position of a ruling group. For this reason, according to the pauline analysis, it was necessary to reduce God to concrete and reachable dimensions, making him a part—although the principal one—of the machinery of the cosmos and of society. From that moment on God is involved in the farce of life. He becomes the jack-of-all-trades to solve all the doubts of the spirit and supply for all the deficiencies of mankind.

This God-jack-of-all-trades gradually loses his functions as man illuminates with his own progress the shadowy zones of ignorance and impotence. Furthermore, the progressive retreat of this "god" is considered a necessary condition for human development or at least an inexorable consequence of this same development. God had become man's rival.

In the history of religions we see how this "deistic" concept takes shape in the assignment of the "sacred" zones and persons. The "sacred" is a space reserved by God for himself, a space to which only the professionals of the cult have access. This is the origin of the "clericalism" found in the ancient religions. This same fact explains the "sacred" character attributable to the exercise of state authority: pharaohs, caesars, and kings sought to belong to the realm of "sacred" jurisdiction, because it contained the secrets and the keys of all the enigmas. Once "god" was presented as the concrete solution for human ignorance and deficiencies, a direct and familiar communication with that "god" gives prestige and preeminence, justifying the predominance of the person or group. Perhaps the real historical origin of the division of humanity in classes was the struggle of those limited to the profane world to seize the secrets and resources hidden within the walled zones of the sacred.

The Bible presents a totally different perspective. In it, the universe appears as an immense, continuous, unified zone. The biblical God has not reserved to himself any specific space, for "his is the fulness of the earth and everything contained therein." The constant affirmation by the prophets, psalmists, and sapiential writers points to this essential idea: God is the only Lord, and in his presence all men have the same degree of essential negativity. Hence, there are no privileged zones of refuge in the universe.

Despite the religious burden which the king or the leader bore in the Israelite theocracy, the state power was completely subject to the unmerciful criticism of the prophets. The prophets were "men of God" but at the same time they were men of the people. They would rise out of the oppressed masses and would courageously undertake to represent them. "Thus says the Lord God. Ho, shepherds of Israel who have been feeding yourselves. Should not the shepherds feed the sheep? But you eat the fat, clothe yourselves with wool, you slaughter the fatling, for you do not feed the sheep. The weak you have not strengthened, the sick you have not healed, the crippled you have not bound up, the stray you have not brought back, the lost you have not sought, and with force and harshness you have ruled them." (Ez 34:2–4)

The biblical God was not in partnership with a ruling class that used the credit of his revered name to their advantage in oppressing the people. Yahweh did not live in comfortable and inaccessible sacred quarters. Rather he would show himself directly to the human masses, and from among them would arise inspired men to struggle valiantly against the alienating attempts of the rulers.

The prophets of Israel were the pioneers in the secular struggle carried out by the inhabitants of the profane to enter the realm of the sacred. According to the biblical religion there is no secret place in the universe or in history where the mysteries of science and power are hidden. God was equidistant from all people, from all human groups, from all individuals. They all have to be silent before him and God is not bound to account for his actions.

The religious man in the Bible does not use God as a working hypothesis to explain the enigmas of knowledge. I insist again on that essential perspective of the whole Bible: God's presence in the progressive evolution of man is a pure grace. It is something totally gratuitous. Hence, the whole Bible is permeated with an insoluble paradox and an answerless question. The anxious "why" of the creature is transmitted from text to text up to the last books of the New Testament, without resolving itself into an accessible and comforting answer for the bourgeois security of an established society.

The psalmists constantly utter the anxious question: "Why have you, oh Lord, forsaken your people? Why have you allowed the sinner to triumph and the just man to be oppressed so that the wicked would sneer at the just?"

The bitter question of the unsuccessful just man also appears in the book of Job. The three friends of Job represent the "deist" attempts to use the God-hypothesis as a coherent and satisfactory explanation for the misfortune of the Idumean noble. However, God himself rejects this solution and resists being used as the explanation of the misfortune. So at the end Job himself acknowledges the transcendence of God and the uselessness of introducing him as an explanation: "Behold I am of small account. What shall I answer thee? I lay my hand on my mouth. I have spoken once, I will not answer; twice, but I will proceed no further" (Job 40:4–5).

The author of Ecclesiastes yields to an ennervating pessimism when he notices the tremendous contradictions of life. Nevertheless he concludes his book by performing a paradoxical somersault of faith: "The end of the matter. All has been heard. Fear God and keep his commandments, for this is the whole duty of man. For God will bring every deed into judgment, with every secret thing, whether good or evil" (Eccl 12:13–14). Again the God-hypothesis has been rejected as the solution to an enigma, and here specifically to the enigma of man's moral behavior. The rejection of the God-hypothesis as the explanation of human behavior reaches its peak in the person of Christ himself. Matthew (27:46–50) and Mark (15:34–37) give us a glimpse of the spiritual darkness of Christ at the moment of his death: "My God, my God, why have you forsaken me?" Those next to the cross allude ironically to the God-hypothesis which evidently is not verified. Christ dies with an anxious cry as he is encircled by the darkness of a mysterious eclipse.

This theme of the "rejection of Christ by God" is found elsewhere in the New Testament. Paul says that "God sent forth his son, born of woman, born under the law to redeem those who were under the law, so that we might receive adoption as his sons." (Gal 4:4–5) In the ancient family adoption was a solution offered by religion and by law to those who had no natural heir to perpetuate their lineage and to insure the continuity of the domestic cult and the transmission of possessions. In order to adopt, it was necessary to have no children. If one had children, they had to be expelled from the family, thus putting an end to any parental jurisdiction over them. This act was called *apokéryxis*. God, in a mysterious and ineffable manner expels his own son from himself in order to adopt the alien. The desolation of the son of God reaches a climax enveloped in the most mysterious of all the paradoxes.

The author of the Epistle to the Hebrews likewise refers to this divine rejection of Christ: "Christ in the days of his flesh offered up prayers and supplication with loud cries and tears to him who was to save him from death, and he was heard for his godly fear. Although he was a Son he learned obedience through what he suffered." (Heb 5:7–8)

We cannot here refer to more biblical passages. But the brief panoramic view we have taken may be an invitation to read the Bible through this lens: the biblical God is never presented as as immanent key to the human problem. God is always a pure grace.

The biblical God is not a rival to the creative autonomy of man

We must next find out if the biblical God is presented as a rival to the creative autonomy of man and his self-realization throughout history.

According to atheistic humanism, especially marxism, the Christian conception of a possible human praxis "stops the movement of history. For the Christian, Jesus came at a given instant to divide time past and future. In his person, the total man is found realized and offered as a model given once for all, leaving out of account the enterprise of gradual progress by which human beings create themselves. From this point, the forward march of mankind has been stripped of its specific meaning. The great effort by which it emerged from nature to forge a new world and to confer on itself a still unknown grandeur, is degraded by acceptance of an imitation, by a movement toward dependence, by attempts to become an image or portrait of a being already real. For a Marxist, the objective is to create and invent a new universe within which man would be not creature but creator, the one responsible for giving himself his own face."[2]

Mury himself puts the point of difference between the marxist conception of the human praxis and Christian soteriology in the right perspective. "Thus," continues the Marxist philosopher, "at the precise moment when the Marxists feel themselves nearest to the believers, they discover what separates them irreducibly from Christianity: they challenge the greatest gift promised to religious minds by faith. They reject the very idea of a grace God can give them. Catholics and Protestants see in this gift and this grace a joyous exultation and a privilege. The strictest teaching of dialectical materialism understands such an achievement simply as a victorious and autonomous action by which man establishes himself through his own decision and effort. No, no gift exists. The glorious and sad history of our species proves that it has conquered quite alone, through the nakedness in which nature left it, the power and strength which are its lot today."[3]

In order to keep our dialogue with marxist humanism from inevitably reaching a dead-end, it is urgent to repeat a point already made, a point which arises from a thorough reading of the Bible and constitutes a constant value for all Christian theology: grace is grace. It is a gratuitous gift which is not given to replace nature, let alone to rival it. Grace does not interfere with nature. It belongs to a different order and cannot be compared, either positively or negatively, with human nature.

The "allergy" to grace which marxist humanism shows can have a satisfactory historical explanation. Indeed, in the history of ideas and of Christian movements there has been a double abuse of the concept of grace.

The first abuse is an attempt to immanentize grace and make it a tyrannical rival of nature. It is a rebirth of the *deus ex machina* of Greco-Roman deism. In the first European church, at Philippi, there was a curious case of this inflation of grace. Some of the

---

[2]G. Mury, *L'Homme chrétien et l'Homme marxiste*, Paris-Geneva, 1964, pp. 56 ff.

[3]G. Mury, *op. cit.*, p. 57.

believers maintained that Christianity was the absolute possessor of all moral values, so that everything that the reflective intellect had patiently accumulated up to then had to be erased completely. The ethical heritage of the Greco-Roman world was basically stoic in origin. St. Paul categorically condemns this attack on the gratuitousness and transcendence of grace. Human reality must be accepted and cannot be prescinded from, he said. Stoic morality has validity in itself. Grace will give a qualifying meaning to that product of human evolution, but it will not squelch the destined development of ascending nature with a magic intervention.[4]

The second abuse is just the opposite extreme: an inflation of transcendence. Grace is presented as something already made and finished, which dwells in a "beyond," where the human spirit must go in order to reach its fullness. In this perspective, human adventure makes no sense. In order to reach the complete investiture of grace in the ultimate "beyond" it would suffice to fulfill perfectly the code completely revealed in the divine message and to accumulate merit. If this were the authentic biblical perspective of grace, Marxist humanism would be right in rejecting a supposedly divine gift which would paralyze and annihilate the epic grandeur of human effort in its ascending evolution and self-creation.

On the contrary, the surprise of the constant evolution of human nature remains intact in the Bible in its effort toward a continuous advancement of itself. The model of this human "advancement" from sin and death to purity and life is, in the pauline exposition, the patriarch Abraham. Abraham by himself could not bring to its fulfillment the existential task assigned by God. This task consisted in being "the father of numberless generations through a son by Sarah." The impossibility of this for Abraham was rooted in the sexual impotence of both spouses. The "judgment" of God is then pronounced upon him. Abraham accepts the judgment as a solution, that is, he "believes in the God who gives life to the dead and calls into existence the things that do not exist." (Rom 4:17) God's judgment, however, does not suppress the reality of the impotence of the elderly couple. It does not create at once a prefabricated Isaac shipped down from heaven. But he "saves" the whole situation by using the natural process. When Paul calls

4Cfr. my own *San Pablo, Cartas de la Cautividad,* Madrid-Rome, 1956, pp. 83 ff.

Isaac "he who was born according to the promise" or "according to the spirit" (Gal 4:23, 29) he is referring to the same biological reality, but as different by reason of the salvific power. Ismael was born without sorrow or glory, "according to the flesh," that is, naturally, as all men are born. In his birth no divine design was revealed which would make it an "event related to salvation history." But Isaac was born "in virtue of a promise." The biological process of his birth was identical to that of Ismael's but by God's design it had been raised to the category of an "event of salvation." It would be an important link in that process leading to the final resurrection which would be the goal of human fullness.[5] Briefly, grace cannot be presented as a source of human alienation, for it neither rivals the laborious and progressive effort of humanity that takes place in historical evolution nor attempts to discourage men in this effort by presenting them with a prefabricated future fulfillment. Grace is not an intruder who is about to eclipse the epic grandeur of Prometheus.

The biblical God despite being gratuitous is salvific

We should, nevertheless, not believe that this qualitative difference between grace and nature constitutes a wall of alienation between them so that grace, despite its transcendent gratuitousness, would fail to be useful and even necessary for the existential fulness of human evolution. Just the opposite. But we must always recognize that it is possible to offer humbly the service of evangelization throughout the world only if we start from the two analyzed presuppositions, viz., the uselessness of the God-hypothesis to explain the human enigma and the self-creative capacity of the human endeavor.

H. Dumery remarks that it was Israel which invented history as a social and religious category, obtaining as a result a remarkable success. "First, it brought about its unity. It thought the continuity of its effort. It fixed itself aims and gave itself tasks. It even made itself boldly the center of humanity's destinies. It did more. To the profit of its culture, and culture in general, it recovered the original experience whence man sets out and to which all men remain bound. By his presence in the world, the human subject

[5]Cfr. my own *Epístola de San Pablo a los Gálatas*, Madrid, 1964, p. 313.

invests all reality with anthropological predicates so that the world
is not made a universe except through and in man's action. From
this point of view Judaism is considered a purposeful humanism
which testifies that the world is not given as a *natural being*, but
as a *cultural* one. The moment it turns up, nature is already
grasped and orientated in a human way. Man appears as the great
cause of meaning. The humanized universe appears as the most
radical, the vastest and the most fruitful of human institutions.
History is no longer what unfolds on the stage of the world. It is
what makes the world turn out a human world. Naturalism is
driven off on all sides. Even nature becomes culture, that is, language, organization, and effectiveness. This is why Israel must be
considered the real inventor of the positiveness of law and morality.
Creation comes from the hands of God, but Adam is its king."[6]

Dumery also observes that throughout the Bible, history appears
as the "revealer" of God. For every pagan civilization it was not
history which revealed God, which expressed the divine, but nature.[7]
But history in the biblical sense is something in a process of becoming and always encloses within itself a future surprise. For that
reason the God of the Bible is a *"Deus absconditus,"* a hidden
God, who must be gradually discovered in an ever new reality,
in every stage of the evolutionary occurrence. In consequence, it is
to man, and only to man, that the task of making this history
through the constant effort of his self-realization falls, thus humanizing nature itself. Now we understand how in biblical religion
the religious dimension of man is precisely his total and complete
responsibility over this humanizing evolution of the cosmos. The
linking of man with God, as appears in the Bible, far from alienating him from his self-creative task, consists precisely in it. Man
cannot give up his own Promethean grandeur without automatically
apostatizing from the God of Abraham, Isaac, and Jacob.

The positive contribution of the biblical message to the self-creative
effort of humanity is exactly the "Christian sense of history." It is
the Bible which in fact has introduced the sense of history as something new in human civilization. From this moment on, men have
begun to think about a common enterprise which would demand
a constant process of human unification. Only after the acceptance

[6]H. Dumery, *Phénoménologie et Religion*, Paris, 1962, p. 9.
[7]H. Dumery, *op. cit.*, p. 6.

of a transcendent God, conceived of as outside and beyond history, was it possible to think of a chronological and spatial unity of the human adventure.

Frequently this sense of history is misunderstood when we reduce it to the eschatological finality of a simple, discontinuous, and prefabricated beyond. Attempting a greater fidelity to the Bible, I would speak of an *eschatologizing* sense of history rather than an *eschatological* one. The eschatologization of the human adventure, far from demanding cessation of man's Promethean effort, is a stimulus and a guarantee of its ascending progress. And this for two reasons: first, because it provides a *meaning*, and second, because it provides a *hidden* meaning, a mystery.

A judgment of the value of the totality of the human enterprise from its humble prehistorical attempts up to the grandeur of the space era can only be formulated *ante factum* from an extrahistorical perspective. That is, from transcendence. Briefly, the meaning of history is a pure grace.

But this "meaning" is "hidden." It is not something made and prefixed. True, it is a guarantee, but also a stimulus for research. As the believer accepts the mystery of history, he only sees a light which goads him to constantly pursue his search of the unknown. The mystery of history, far from supressing the surprise of the progressive novelty of human self-realization, makes it both desirable and possible. Thus we understand that a religious community which pretends that its rigid institutionalization has exhausted the worldly manifestations of the mystery of history is committing the sacrilege of attempted prevention of the progressive manifestation of the *Deus absconditus*. Every retreat of Christian communities within themselves to defend behind walls the inheritance entrusted to them implies a tremendous lack of faith in the necessary surprise of *Deus semper maior*.

Finally this hidden sense, this mystery, of history—the real essence of the message revealed in the Bible—is a great antidote against the danger of having a caste, a nation, a group, or a person take over the reins of human evolution. History has meaning insofar as God is its only Lord. The Bible, at the same time that it intro- duced the magic and attractive word "messianism," presented Christ as the only Messiah, the only Lord who could truly rule the course of history. If, despite this unique and absolute lordship of Christ, the churches themselves have frequently fallen into the temptation of messianic usurpation, what guarantees can we have for the future, once we do away with this leveling factor?

"Christianity," writes Paul Ricoeur, "has an instinctive distrust of systematic philosophies of history which would like to provide us with the key to intelligibility. One has to choose between system or mystery. The mystery of history puts me on guard against theoretical practical, intellectual, and political fanaticisms. Faith in meaning, but in a meaning hidden from history, is thus both the courage to believe in a profound significance of the most tragic history (and therefore a feeling of confidence and resignation in the very heart of conflict) and a certain rejection of system and fanaticism, a sense of the open."[8]

[8]P. Ricoeur, op. cit., pp. 95–96.

CHAPTER 3

MAN'S GUILT IN THE ECLIPSE OF GOD

In his letter to the Romans St. Paul makes a deep analysis of the essential absence of God from the "believing" or religious society of his time. Paul divides the world into two great blocs, Jewish and Greek, both of which were certainly religious societies.

Paul recognizes the validity and authenticity of the religious tendency in each bloc which had given birth to a certain type of religiosity. He now shows up in the middle of the unknown world —Rome—to proclaim officially the "good news"—the "Gospel"— that is, the great salvific event. The content of this proclamation is a "power of God for salvation to everyone who has faith" (Rom 1:16).

"Salvation" is a very rich concept in the whole of biblical litera- ture. "This word signifies all the blessings which God alone can give in answer to the need and longing of man, who is oppressed and in anguish in face of a destiny which sharpens his need of super- natural beatitude in proportion as it does nothing to satisfy it."[1]

The biblical man is the concrete, integral, bodily man. Death is an attempt on this human integrity and only by overcoming it will man be able to consider his existential fullness as perfectly achieved. The "gospel" is then the valid and official proclamation on the part of God of the great event of salvation. Man will be able to achieve his human fullness effectively. He is not a desperate Sisyphus who struggles upward in vain carrying a useless burden on his shoulders.

[1]Franz J. Leenhardt, *The Epistle to the Romans*, Lutterworth Press, London, 1961, p. 47.

God offers his "salvation" to every believer.

What does "believing" mean?

Throughout the whole of the Old Testament, "belief reveals man's vital position with respect to God who is manifested as the liberator of the chosen people. Some partial aspects, seemingly included and unified in that totality, are: (a) the knowledge and recognition of Yahweh, of his salvific and ruling power as revealed in the history of Israel: (b) trust in his promise (with reverential fear); (c) obedience to the precepts of Yahweh. This aspect of trust is generally (not always) more evident and in some ways more predominant in the faith of the Old Testament. But the vital, integral reality of this faith includes the *total* affirmation (on the part of the human faculties) with regard to the recognition and veneration of Yahweh as the only savior of Israel. Through faith man finds support in the divine word and promises—*in God himself*—and enters upon a vital communion with him. But that faith refers to a given content, which is more or less implicitly in favor of the chosen people, and this content implies man's submission to the will of God. To *believe* in the Old Testament is to nod in assent to the word, promises, and precepts of Yahweh."[2]

In Paul "faith" is still considered as a "leaning on" the divine promises of salvation. For that reason, the pauline dialectic of salvation through faith starts with a *midrash* on Abraham, the father of all believers (Gal 3, Rom 4).

The "work" of Abraham, his "existential task" designed by God, was to be the father of many nations through Isaac (Rom 4:17; Gen 17:5; Is 48:13). The elderly patriarch could not bring this "task" to its fulfillment by himself for he and Sarah were sexually as good as dead (Rom 4:19). God, however, appears to Abraham and promises him the capacity to fulfill the assignment. The God who promises is the very God who "gives life to the dead and calls into existence the things that did not exist" (Rom 4:17). "Abraham believes" in this God, creator and giver of life (Rom 4:17); that is, the weak man whose vital task was frustrated *leans* on or finds support in the absolute and vivifying Being.

This is precisely what faith is: "to lean on God-life" and not, on the contrary, to "weaken in faith considering his own mortality" (Rom 4:19). Paul's description is clear and concise. Man-by-himself cannot accomplish his "work," his "existential task," since "death" limits fatally his "life" and "sin" his "doing good."

But God—as in the case of Abraham—has shown himself to man and has established a salvific dialogue with him. This dialogue in the Old Testament was a simple promise (Gal 3), but "now" it has become a "primordial reality." God *promised* man "salvation" in the Old Testament, that is, the existential fulness of victory over sin and death. In the New Testament he *already offers* the beginning of this salvation. There is already *a* man, the first and foremost, who has already achieved this existential fullness. This man is the Man, the true Adam, Jesus Christ.

As a result, the theme of the divine-human dialogue of faith is precisely the resurrection: Christ's resurrection as a consummated fact and as guarantee and cause of the future resurrection of the believers. "If you confess with your lips that Jesus is Lord and believe in your heart that God raised him from the dead, you will be saved" (Rom 10:9). This "salvation" refers essentially to the resurrection of the believer. "But we would not have you ignorant, brethren, concerning those who are asleep, that you may not grieve, as others do who have no hope. For since we believe that Jesus died and rose again, even so, through Jesus God will bring with him those that have fallen asleep" (1 Thes 4:13–14).

In Chapter 15 of his first letter to the Corinthians Paul develops this theme at great length. The content of Christian preaching as offered to the believers is essentially the event of Christ's resurrection. This same resurrection of Christ has no special importance from the point of view of history-in-itself, but precisely by the intimate connection that it has with man's "existential task." The resurrection of Christ is the "primordial beginning" (*aparxe*, v. 20, 23) of the eschatological resurrection of the believers.

As we see, "to believe" is an act that commits and involves man totally. In the first place, it is a cognoscitive operation. It is the acceptance of a proclamation made by God or in the name of God having to do with an offer of "salvation," but this "cognizance" implies a vital position of "recognition." Recognition of man's own incapacity to reach the existential fullness, and of the power—*dynamis*—of God to bring man to the total achievement of his destiny. Therefore there is a close connection between "believing" and "salvation." Faith is a full acceptance of God's salvation offer.

The conclusion is clear. This offer of salvation, officially proclaimed—"evangelized"—is destined only for the believer, "for every believer" *(panti to pisteuonti)*. Vis-à-vis this offer of salvation there is no valid position but that of the "believer."

What are the limits set by Paul to this divine offer of salvation, and consequently to the possibility of a position of faith on the part of men?

All men can believe

In the first place, he acknowledges that the fact of the actual proclamation of salvation, the "gospel," is destined for every "believer, whether Jewish or Greek." But the question always remains about non-Jewish humanity (in Paul's actual thought, the "Greek") who had not even heard the previous announcement of salvation of the Old Testament revelation. What relationship did God have with purely historical man, with the man who had not received any supernatural message from heaven? This is the theme developed by Paul in great length in the next passage (Rom 1:17 to 2:16).

He starts with a highly concentrated formula which contains the thesis he will develop shortly. "For in the event of the proclamation of the Gospel, God's favorable judgment is revealed from faith to faith, as it is written, 'he who through faith is righteous shall live'" (1:17). The verse is dominated by a causal conjunction indicating that it is a justification of the previous phrase; that is, the Gospel is a proclamation of the power-of-God-for-salvation for every believer, precisely because his favorable judgment is revealed in it.

The word used by Paul, *dikaiosyne*, has a very concrete meaning which cannot be translated by the expression "justice." There are many passages in the Old Testament where the "justice" of Yahweh consisted precisely in bringing "salvation" to his people (Is 45:21; 46: 13 LXX; 51:5 LXX; Ps 36:7, 11; 40:11; 71:2, 15; 103:4; 98:2; Mic 7:19). We find the same idea in the Hymns of Qumram: "You forgive wickedness and purify man of his sin through your justice" (Hymn IV, 33), and the Rule of the Community: "I say to

God: my justice! And to the Highest: Author of my good!" (RC X, 33; cf. *ibid.* X, 15–17; *Doc. Damsc.*, 20.20).

It is therefore God's "favorable judgment" passed on mankind, without which mankind would end up in total failure.

These two chapters of the letter to the Romans are considered the most important single passage defining the meaning of God with respect to man-in-himself. Vatican I uses it as the primary source for its dogmatic affirmation on the knowledge of God (Constitution on Catholic Faith, Chap. 2, DS 3004). Paul starts off from the necessity of a salvation for man, of a meaning for his life, of a human outcome in a destiny of existential fullness.

God appears on the human horizon as the bearer of total salvation. Paul will shortly develop this theme of God's presence, starting from man's inadequacy when he sets out to develop his own existence. That is why he says that in *it*, that is, in the gospel (the proclamation of the Good News) the "favorable judgment of God is revealed." The word used by Paul, *apokalyptetai*, is not properly translated by the modern expression "to reveal," an expression which has a definite intellectual nuance. As commonly used in the greek version of the Old Testament it usually corresponds to the hebrew *galáh*—i.e., not to "an intellectual type of knowledge, but rather to an intuitive contact with what is hidden in transcendence, especially when the term is used to mean an immanentization of pre-existing transcendental realities."[3]

This *apokalypsis* is more than a "revelation"; it is an "apparition" or a breaking in of the transcendent into the immanent. In Is 56:1 "justice" and "salvation," and "to come" and "to reveal" (that is, to appear) are placed in a close parallel. "Thus says the Lord. Keep justice and do righteousness, for soon my salvation will come and my deliverance be revealed." The "Gospel" is precisely this: a salvific event which consists in the appearance in the midst of history of a divine judgment passed on human existence for its "salvation." This appearance of the judgment of God's savior, says Paul, is produced "from faith to faith" (ex *pisteos eis pistin*). The pauline expression has been understood in many ways: from faith to faith, that is, in continuous progress; from the faith of the preacher to the faith of the listeners; from *fides informata* to *fides formata*;[4]

[3]A. Oepke, *Theologisches Wörterbuch zum Neuen Testament*, III, p. 579.
[4]St. Thomas, III, 9, XLIV, 1.

from the ancient faith to the new faith (Tertullian); and totally
leaning on faith from one end to another.

If we refer only to the parallel passages (2 Cor 3:18; Ps 84:8; Jer
9:2), we have to admit first a certain sense of local progress. The
apostles "are reflecting the glory of God, changing from one degree
of glory to another" (*apo doxes eis doxan*, 2 Cor 3:18). Paul admits
that the "economy of the law" allowed its greatest representative,
Moses, to reflect in his face a divine glory, but "in the economy of
the spirit" the apostles, its authorized representatives, also reflect
the likeness of God, but "changing from one degree of glory to
another," that is, changing from a "fading" (*katargoumenen*, v.7)
glory to an "excellent" (v.10) and "permanent" (v.11) glory.

In Psalm 84 a pilgrim gradually approaches the Temple of
Jerusalem singing and "moving from hill to hill until finally God
will be seen in Sion," on the highest hill where the Temple is
located. In both cases the *apokalypsis* is like a final term, the explosion in the meridian of a progressive luminous process.

In 2 Cor 3, Paul through a skillfully done *midrash* on Ex 34:29–35
compares himself, the Apostle, with Moses. Moses received the
oracles directly from God which were made sensible in the glory
that shone in his face. The apostles also received the gospel directly
from God and shine permanently in order to radiate that divine
light to all the faithful (2 Cor 3:18).

Moses had to cover his face with a veil so that God's light would
not blind the Israelites. Paul continues the rabbinic subtlety of the
midrash: that veil still covers the face of "Moses" as he is read in
the synagogues. The Jews possess the true word of God, but for
them it is a hidden, covered, veiled word. As soon as the veil is
removed they will also be illuminated. In Galatians 1:15 Paul
remembers that he too had the Son of God in his hands, as contained in the old revelation: "But when he who set me apart
before I was born and had called me through his grace, was pleased
to reveal (*apokalypsai*) his Son in me in order that I might preach
him among the gentiles." "In him" (in Paul) Christ was hidden,
veiled by Jewish incomprehension and pride. In the substratum
of Paul's existence all the realities, including his apostolic vocation, as decreed by God from his first moment, were already
there, but they were hidden and veiled. There came the moment
when divine Mercy wanted to "lift up the veil," to "unveil" the
Son of God that was hidden in the Rabbi Paul.

Likewise in Psalm 84 that "appearance" of the great Temple on the highest hill climaxed a slow progress of the salvific power of God, proclaimed in the Chapel, and supposes a progress along the mysterious route of faith. Paul opposes the "salvific judgment" of God, proclaimed in the Chapel, and supposes a progress along some sort of "faith." Man acknowledges his weakness and gets ready to lean on the *dynamis* (power) of God who offers his salvation.

Then, as the salvific judgment of God has followed an ascending route in its manifestation up to the *apokalypsis* of the gospel, likewise the human acceptance has traveled a progressive road, marked in all its stages by faith, from the incipient and dark faith of the man who meets God through "the reflective contemplation of his works" (Rom 1:20) to the illumined and complete faith of him who receives the message of Christ's resurrection as the main event and guarantee of the universal resurrection or human fulness.

No wonder Paul qualifies the religious attitudes of "natural" man as a kind of faith. In the pauline concept, and in general in the biblical concept, faith is not specified by the acceptance of a verbal message (even though it often includes it) but by an attitude of "leaning on." As we will see shortly, Paul defines the relations of man and God in terms of "meeting," of a call on the part of God who offers man a salvation, which he alone could not achieve. Men then must acknowledge their weakness and accept the divine help. This is faith according to the biblical concept.

To stress even further the intimate connection between the human act of "believing-leaning" and the divine act of salvation, Paul quotes a passage from Habacuc (2:4): "He who through faith is righteous shall live." Salvation is promised to the Israelites in an anxious moment of their national life, precisely because they are not proud, as the Chaldeans, but give themselves to Yahweh and expect everything from him, especially that concrete salvation for which they long so insistently. The life that Yahweh promises is certainly a temporal one, the survival of Israel as a people. Likewise the man who "accepts" God, who meets him, expects that some day he "will live." "To live" is the supreme expression of salvation desired by man and offered by God. But this tendency to life originates in faith. "He who through faith is righteous shall live." The acceptance-faith is the starting point on a road that will lead to life, salvation, and human fulness.

All men can culpably cease to believe

Once Paul has established the thesis of God's "favorable" judgment brought to its fulness in the proclamation of the good news, he examines the opposite of this proposition. When man does not "believe," that is, does not accept humbly this salvation that God offers, there also "appears" an "unfavorable judgment" of God: "The wrath of God is revealed from heaven against all ungodliness and wickedness of men who by their wickedness suppress the truth" (Rom 1:18).

This "unfavorable judgment" is called anthropomorphically "wrath." In many biblical texts both expressions—"wrath" and "justice"—are mentioned in a parallel and corresponding form. If a man rejects salvation and then turns to recognize and to lean on God, God returns his "justice," that is, he passes a saving judgment on him. (Mic 7:9; 6:5; Ps 85:4–8; Ps 69:25–29, 30–37, etc.) Paul insists in his concept of "fulness" as applied to the event of the proclamation of the good news. Now (in the Gospel) we also "discover" the unfavorable judgment of God. Guilt and "unfaithfulness" on the part of men have been increasing.

In the period before the gospel (always understood objectively as the proclamation of the divine offer of salvation) there was a presence of God before men, and consequently an acceptance on the part of men—a "faith"—in that initial encounter with God. The gospel is a meridian explosion of this encounter, the *apokalypsis*. Likewise parallel to the "faith" of historical man, there was also "resistance" and "unbelief" which now, in contrast with the "gospel," reaches its climax. Paul acknowledges the small degree of responsibility of pre- or extra-evangelical man and even says that that was a time of "tolerance" (*paresis*) of past sins, and of patient waiting for God (*anoxe*) (Rom 3:25; cfr. Acts 17:30: "times of ignorance").

However, even before the evangelical *apokalypsis*, God also passed an "unfavorable judgment" on men. And here begins the pauline description of the non-Jewish world, of what we can call in modern terminology "natural man." These men even had in fact a knowledge of truth, a meeting with the divine, but were not faithful to the light that was offered to them, and went so far as to "suppress the truth" with their wickedness.

Paul does not mean to draw a totally negative picture of pagan morality, in order to present the gospel as the only solution for its total purification. Quite the opposite. He recognizes that the pagans are responsible for a situation of "unpiety" and "immorality." He does not want to say either that *all* pagans had fallen into a lamentable situation or that *all* were responsible for it. He only wants to show that in the pagan world there had been a culpable degradation of the divine manifestation. In the following verses Paul presents a phenomenological analysis of religious sociology in the pagan or "natural" world, referring concretely to the Greco-Roman world.

The previous assertion was that God's unfavorable judgment with respect to the religious degradation of the pagan world is justified because that "degradation" was not purely intellectual but caused in great part by an "immoral" attitude. Paul's expression is strong and significant. "They suppress the truth with their wickedness." To prove his assertion the apostle analyzes the contemporary religious situation. He starts by recognizing that "what can be known about God is plain to them" (Rom 1:19). But this presence of God in the purely human world is not conceived of by Paul as a philosophical or cognoscitive relation of subject to object, but as a call to man on the part of a personal God "because God has shown it to them." *(ibid.)* It is the living God of Abraham, Isaac, and Jacob and not the Idea-God, pure object of a philosophical speculation.

However, this active manifestation of the personal God is not made through a supernatural utterance (as it was with the prophets of Israel) but through the reflective power of man: "for ever since the creation of the world, his invisible nature, namely his eternal power and deity, has been clearly perceived in the things that have been made" (1:20).

And exactly what is that "which can be known about God," that "invisible"? Paul points it out explicitly: "his eternal power and deity." *(ibid.)* *Dynamis* in Paul undoubtedly has the meaning it has constantly in the Old Testament, the power of God operating in the midst of history which conforms and models history itself and impresses upon it a positive finality: a salvation. This power of God is concentrated in the Christ-event, and above all in his victory over death.[5] For that reason he has clearly affirmed in the

[5] Cfr. W. Grundmann, *Theologisches Wörterbuch zum Neuen Testament*, II, 307.

presentation of his thesis that "the gospel is a power of God for salvation" (Rom 1:16). "The word of the Cross is for salvation, a power of God" (1 Cor 1:18).

This "power of God" is balanced constantly by human weakness (*astheneia*). Christ himself mysteriously assumed the weak condition of man (Phil 2:7–8; 2 Cor 5:21; Rom 8:3; Gal 3:13; 4:4) and "died as a result of that weakness" (*ex astheneias*, 2 Cor 13:4). The human weakness he had taken on himself led him inescapably to its existential breakdown, namely, death. Christ did not, however, become incarnate in the weakness of man, as a purely romantic gesture of solidarity, but rather in order to begin this "solidarity" in Christ as the salvific action of the "power of God." He lives by the power of God" (*ibid.*). Therefore the "climax of the power of God" (Eph 1:19) is manifested in the "working of his great might which he accomplished in Christ when he raised him from the dead"(Eph 1:19–20). Therefore "faith" which is an acknowledgement of weakness and acceptance of the salvation offered by the "power of God" refers essentially to the great event of God, namely, the resurrection of Christ, "first fruit" and guarantee of the resurrection of the believer (1 Thes 4:14; 1 Cor 14:15, 17; 2 Cor 4:13–14; Rom 10:9; Col 2:12; Eph 1:19–20; 2 Tim 2:8).

Precisely in the same epistle to the Romans Paul develops in great detail this correlation between "human weakness," "divine power" and "salvation-faith." Abraham was a "weak" man, that is, lacking "life" and "power." Both dimensions were honestly acknowledged. On the one hand he presented himself before God with empty hands, with a humble confession of his previous pagan life: he could "not work but trusted him who justified the ungodly" (Rom 4:5). On the other hand, "he considered his own body as good as dead, because he was about a hundred years old, and likewise he considered the barrenness of Sarah's womb" (4:19). Abraham lived humbly (and conscious of his weakness) and from it he went to meet God who offered him "salvation." God appeared to him effectively as the bearer of his *power*, the power of salvation (4:20).

This dialectic of "human weakness-divine power" plays a very important role in Paul's theology. "I will all the more gladly boast of my weakness so that the power of God may rest upon me" (2 Cor 12:9). "But we have this treasure in earthen vessels, to show that the transcendent power belongs to God and not to us" (2 Cor 4:7). "I can do all things in him who strengthens me" (Phil 4:13).

The power of God, therefore, is the adequate answer to the profound sense of weakness and insufficiency that characterizes human existence. It is not a cold and speculative reasoning about the origin of being, or of beings, but specifically a vital experience of the creature itself upon reaching a reflective stage in its evolution. Man is a being thrown into life. Some superior "power" rules over his existence offering him fullness and meaning. This search for the meaning of existence and fullness of destiny—according to the formidable pauline analysis—is the starting point of the encounter of man with God.

This power of God—Paul goes on—is "eternal." It is something beyond the reach of time. It dominates history and covers it from one end to the other. Next to the "power of God," parallel with it, is his "divinity. The *theiotes* is the nature of God: it is what God manifests and what gives him the right to divine veneration. In the imperial cult, so popular in the Greco-Roman world, the *theiotes* refers to the magnificence of Caesar's glory. It was said about Maximinus Daza: "the divinity of our Lord is very bright" *(e theiotes tou despotou emon epelampsen*[6]).

Man thrown into life acknowledges his weakness and the insufficiency of his cosmic context, and from there he rises to meet a superior and personal being, who appears to him as salvific power and an immanent lord.

In order to understand accurately the depth of Paul's thought, we have to start from the presupposition that for the apostle the natural "manifestation" of God to man has such validity in itself that it can commit him and push him to a fundamental choice in his life. Man, in fact, after this "manifestation" of God is "without excuse" (Rom 1:20).

Paul does not refer to every man in particular, but to the Greco-Roman world as it was in history, which for him symbolizes and universalizes the position of natural man arrived at a certain degree of cultural maturity. It was a fact that in this world, helped only by the resources of their natural faculties, men had arrived at a remarkable knowledge of God. That knowledge, despite its obvious obscurity and imperfection, offered a sufficient degree of light on which to base moral behavior. For a better understanding of Paul's appreciation of the human effort in its search for God we complement the

[6]Ditt. Syll., 3–900, 20; cfr. H. Kleinknecht, *Theologisches Wörtenbuch zum Neuen Testament*, III, 123.

reading of this chapter from Romans with two other pauline passages on the subject, as related in Acts (14:15–17 and 17:22–31).[7]

In Acts, chapter 17, Paul recognizes that the Athenians are very "religious men" (17:22) but in a delicate way lets them know that their religiosity (although to their advantage) is imperfect. For this purpose he makes use of a magnificent rhetorical device which happened to be available as a result of the discovery of an altar dedicated "to an unknown God." (17:23) Fr. E. des Places proposed recently a reading which is philologically correct and—in our opinion —more in consonance with the proximate context of the epistle: "to the unknowable God."[8] Indeed the Greeks had a very live consciousness of the divine transcendence which they expressed with a form of reverential fear regarding "the nameability" of God. To give God a name was like daring to define and contain the immensity of a being or beings felt to be superior to human and worldly contingency. The theme is frequent in Plato. "But regarding the names of the gods, could we study them—as you were doing in the case of Zeus a few minutes ago—to see how accurately they have been named?—(Socrates): By Zeus, Hermogenes, if we had sense, we would recognize that there is one way, and only one, to do this, namely, to affirm that of the gods we know nothing, neither of them nor of the names, by which they call themselves, for it is clear that they use the true names. A second kind of correctness could be to call them, as is customary in prayers, by whatever names and patronymics are pleasing to them, since we know no other."[9]

"My awe, Protarchus, in respect to the names of the gods is always beyond the greatest human fear."[10] "Now to discover the maker and father of this universe were a task indeed; and having discovered him, to declare him unto all men were a thing impossible." (*ton poieten kai patera toude tou pantos eurein te ergon kai*

---

[7]It has been recently pointed out against Dibelius that there is a close connection between these two texts of Luke and the chapter to the Romans. Cfr. P. Dupon, *Le problème du livre des Actes 'apres travaux récents*, Louvain, 1950.

[8]Fr. E. des Places, *Au Dieu inconnu* (Acts 71:23), *Biblica*, 40(1959), p. 793–99. The "*gnoston*" of Ro 1:19 has that nuance of "knowability," "what can be known."

[9]Plato, *Cratylus*, 400D; transl. by H. N. Fowler, Will. Heinemann Ltd., London, 1926, p. 63.

[10]Plato, *Philebus*, 12C, transl. by H. N. Fowler, Heinemann Ltd., London, 1925, p. 207.

euronta eis pantas adynaton legein.)[11] This text was very popular among the Fathers.[12]

This sensitivity to divine transcendence is expressed especially in the prayers to the divinity often found in the poets. "Hear me, oh Lord, whoever you are!"[13] "Zeus, whoever he is, if this be a name acceptable, by this name I will call him."[14] "Zeus, Zeus, what do I say? Where do I begin?"[15] "O Earth's Upbearer, thou whose throne is Earth, Who'er thou be, O past our finding out, Zeus be thou Nature's Law, or Mind of Man, Thee I invoke; for treading soundless paths to Justice' goal thou bring'st all mortal things."[16]

"The different names given to the supreme being can be reduced to philosophical systems in fashion at the time of Euripides. The god that rules the earth and sits upon it is the air, the first principle of Diogenes of Apollonia. The necessity of rain in nature reminds us surely of Heraclitus' doctrine and finally the term itself of *nous* reflects the influence of Anaxagoras."[17]

Introducing himself into this climate of anxious search for the divinity, Paul claims to take advantage of the positive aspect of the search and to complement it with his "proclamation." "What therefore you worship as unknown, this I proclaim to you" (Acts 17:23). It is not a new god ("an unknown god") which Paul is going to proclaim, but a new aspect of the divinity, which in the "natural" world was unknowable, and he is going to proclaim specifically "the god that made the world and everything in it" (Acts 17:24). "The living God who made the heaven and the earth and the sea and all that is in them" (Acts 14:15). This is the aspect (*touto* in neuter gender) that they adore without knowing it. This is the name of God that the worshippers do not dare to utter because they are aware of the mystery that resides beyond the frontiers of human knowledge. It is the God-savior who gives to all

[11]Plato, *Timaeus*, 28C, transl. by R. G. Burg, Heinemann Ltd., London, 1929, p. 51.

[12]Cfr. A. J. Festugière, *Contemplation et vie contemplative selon Platon*, Paris, 1936, pp. 94, 109 note 3.

[13]Homer, *Odyssey*, V, 445.

[14]Aeschylus, *Agamemnon*, 160–162, transl. by Louis MacNeice, Faber and Faber Ltd., London, 1955.

[15]Aeschylus, *Choephori*, 855.

[16]Euripides, *The Daughters of Troy*, 883–88, transl. by A. S. Way, Heinemann Ltd., London, p. 427.

[17]E. Parmentier-H. Grégoire, *Euripide*, Paris, 1925, p. 64.

men "life and breath and everything" (17:25). God who "did good and gave from heaven rains and fruitful seasons, satisfying your hearts with food and gladness" (14:17). Paul establishes an equation between the "god-benefactor" whom men knew vaguely and worshiped and the "God that creates" whom he announces and proclaims. Creation is a positive datum of supernatural revelation.

That "manifestation" of God to the "natural" man was certainly imperfect and Paul describes it with vigorous lines that determine exactly the sociological context in which the search for God took place. "To seek God in the hope that they might feel after and find him" (17:27).[18]

It is an active search. It is the answer to the sound of God's steps as he walks through his created works. Paul recognizes that the search for God is painful and difficult, like the anxious, careful groping of a blind man in the vacillating hope of finding something of which he has heard an imprecise and undetermined rumor.

The God "capable of being found" is, however, "not far from each of us. For in him we live, and move and have our being" (17:27–28). This triplet ("to live," "to move," and "to have our being") is frequent in greek philosophy and specially in Stoicism.[19] Paul could have taken it directly from some popular form of stoicism or perhaps through the undeniable hellenistic influence with which the diaspora synagogues were tinged, as can be seen in the Wisdom Literature of the Bible.

Despite this reference to hellenistic literature, we cannot deny that the whole phrase has a certain biblical substratum which will give us the key to the authentic pauline thought. The binomial "search-find" applied to Yahweh frequently shows up in the prophets and in the psalms. Both concepts refer to a radically religious position, whose greatest expression is prayer and liturgy. "Seek the Lord, while he may be found. Call upon him while he is near" (Is 55:6).

In this text, by virtue of the synthetic parallelism, we see that "to seek" is more or less a synonym of "to call," and "to find" is on

18The expression ei ara has this complicated nuance of hope and doubt. Num 22:1; Mk 11:13; Acts 8:22. Pselafao means to feel after, to touch, and here there is a clear allusion to the groping search of a blind person. The insecurity of the search is stressed even further by the optative forms pselafeseian and heuroien.

19Tim. 37c,6; Sophist. 248E, 7–8; Phaedrus, 245E; Plutarch, De Gen. Socr., 519B.

the same level as "to be near." "The Lord is near to all who call upon him" (Ps 145:18). "They cry for help, the Lord hears and delivers them out of all their troubles. The Lord is near to the broken-hearted and saves the crushed in spirit" (Ps 34:17–18). "Let the oppressed see it and be glad. You who seek God, let your heart revive! For the Lord hears the needy, and does not despise his own that are in bonds" (Ps 69:32–33). "Seek the Lord and his strength, seek his presence continually" (Ps 105:4). The psalm begins with an invitation to thanksgiving: "Give thanks to the Lord. Call on his name."

Therefore, the "nearness" of God has no purely eschatological or apocalyptic meaning but has the nuance of the insistent presence of the divine in human reality. God is near and "can be sought" by men. This search is not purely intellectual but predominantly religious. It is prayer. Paul himself, following this Old Testament thought, exhorts to prayer using the motive of God's proximity (Phil 4:5).[20]

In summary, for Paul the knowledge that natural man has of God is imperfect and vacillating, full of undeniable imperfections, but it can determine a consequent moral behavior. Man cannot so easily rid himself of this divine pressure on the pretext that its presence is obscure and anxious. On the contrary, he must strive in this painful search, recognizing his own weakness and attempting to accept the salvation offered by the transcendent.

On this presupposition of the existence of a knowledge of God (although obscure, imperfect and unsure) Paul passes a judgment on the consequent degradation: "so they are without excuse, for although they knew God they did not honor him as God or give thanks to him" (1:20–21). God's manifestations in the pagan world demanded a position of acceptance on the part of man (a "faith") that consists in acknowledging the divine sovereignty from his own weakness ("to honor") and in leaning "gratefully" on the offer of salvation that God provides. Paul does not speak of *all* men and each individual man. He starts from a known and evident fact: men have known God.

The somber description the apostle gives of the more depressing vices of the pagan world cannot be taken simply as a pessimistic

[20]Cfr. my own commentary.

view of surrounding reality. His intention is much deeper and
essentially "theological." He is attempting to explain the coexistence
of a "religious profession" with grossly immoral behavior. It was
common in some areas, especially civilized, to find a repugnant
mingling of an ornate religious cult with a total perversion of morals.
Indeed, right next to the temples themselves the most degrading
habits would flourish under the guise of rites protected by religious
myths formulated in such a way as to encourage the practice of vice.

This is the starting point for the profound sociological analysis
that Paul makes of the origin of atheism in the non-Jewish religious
world. Man who has had this dark encounter with God should
have adopted a humble attitude of recognition of his own weakness
and of anxious and hesitating search in a prayerful attitude. Had
he done so, his moral life would be much more pure. Paul does
does not deny that among pagans there were and there could have
been many authentically religious men who carried out this search
for God sincerely. "On the day of wrath when God's righteous
judgment will be revealed he will render to every man according to
his works" (Rom 2:5–6). And this "final judgment" will fall
indiscriminately upon Jews and Gentiles alike. Both will be bene-
ficiaries of the fulness of salvation and for both likewise it will be
possible to end up in total failure. "There will be tribulation and
distress for every human being that does evil, the Jew first and also
the Greek. But glory and honor and peace for everyone that does
good, the Jew first and also the Greek. For God shows no partiality"
(Rom 2:9–10).

The problem is thus presented on the presupposition of a conscious encounter between man and God. Carried away by his pride
man accepts God conditionally and undertakes the difficult task of
taming the divine. He does not renounce his knowledge (his
"theodicy") of which he explicitly boasts: "And claiming to be wise
they become fools" (Rom 1:22). In a culpable way he tries to
change the transcendent gift, thus degrading it: "They exchange the
glory of the immortal God for images resembling mortal men, or
birds, or animals, or reptiles" (Rom 1:23). This "exchange" is
considered by Paul as culpable at least in those who started it
consciously thereby inaugurating a sinful structure that contaminates
the whole mass collectively.

This, according to the apostle, is the origin of atheism in the non-Jewish religious world: the culpable degradation of an initial theology of the transcendent into a "theodicy" of the immanent. A personal and transcendent God, obscure and difficult as he was, was too uncomfortable and demanded an adventurous attitude of "faith" that human pride could not accept humbly. For that reason at the very beginning not daring to dispose of him entirely, men attempted to immanentize him, totally commiting him to their farce and attempting bribery by the offer of the first place of honor in their orgy.

This is the beginning of the death of God. God has ceased to be God. He has been made instead the constitutional president of the human republic. Theology has become "theodicy." God is the explanation (skillfully manipulated) of all the enigmas and the justification of all modes of behavior. Paul gives a list of the most repugnant vices of the pagan world (Rom 1:26–32), not simply to show the state of corruption, but to make clear that that situation had been culpably provoked by some "intellectuals" who, having been able to draw high moral consequences from the knowledge of God, "suppressed the truth" (1:18), and attempted to tame the divine, to the point of enclosing it sacrilegiously in the context of their degraded life.

The result of this sinful situation is death: "those who knowing God's decree do such things, deserve to die" (Rom 1:32). "Death" in Paul, as in the whole Bible, has a full sense. It is not only biological death, but the total failure of human existence, without a possibility of emergence. "Death-in-Christ" is not properly speaking death, but "sleep," for it is a transition to the future resurrection (Rom 6:3–11; 1 Thes 4:13–15; 1 Cor 15:18–20).

All this must be seen in context. Since Paul's rebuke is not addressed primarily to the human masses, who in great degree practised those vices without fault of their own, but against the "intellectuals" responsible for that situation, he attacks these latter violently: "not only those who do such things, but those who approve them, deserve to die" (Rom 1:32). The verb used—*syneudokein*—is frequently employed in pauline literature to mean intellectual responsibility for other people's actions (Lk 11:48; Acts 8:1; 22:20; 1 Cor 7:12–13).

The intellectuals of pagan society enclosed themselves in the solitude of their "gnosis" and believed that they were following their conscience, as they disapproved in their hearts those excesses but without committing themselves in public as teachers and spiritual leaders. In other words, they failed to unveil the falseness of the promiscuous coexistence of pseudo-religion and immorality. Paul deals with a theme that is today very much alive when he speaks as "denouncer-prophet" of moral deviations. In 1 Cor 9:16–17 he acknowledges that "preaching the gospel gives me no ground for boasting, for necessity is laid upon me. Woe to me if I do not preach the gospel." To the Galatians he addresses a severe rebuke: "If anyone is preaching to you a gospel contrary to the one you have received, let him be accursed. Am I now seeking the favor of men or God? Or am I trying to please men? If I were still pleasing men, I would not be a servant of Christ" (Gal 1:9–10). Perhaps in the *substratum* of pauline thought the memory of Balaam was still vivid. The prophet could not help uttering the divine oracle even thought he would become *persona non grata* to his fellow men. At one moment Balaam even offers sacrifices in an effort to persuade God to curse Israel (Num 23:24). Likewise when Roboam and the people besieged in the city prayed to God that he might grant them victory and salvation, they could not persuade God to uphold their cause.[21] This sense of attempting to convince God to make him agree to human desires is also found in classical literature: "gifts persuade gods" (*dora theous peithei*.)[22] Paul affirms his unconditional submission to the divine norm and not only does he not seek the favor of men but he does not even attempt to persuade God not to impel him to "anathematize" the innovating Galatians. He is the "servant of Christ" and therefore he can only "please" or "serve" Christ. The title of "servant of Christ" appears in Paul in a context that we could call apostolic (Rom 1:1; Col 4:12; Cfr. Jas 1:1; 2 Pet 1:1; Jud 1). The title "servant of God" is equivalent to "worshipper" or devoted to God. It is often employed in a context we could call prophetic and thus the person whom God has given a special task related to the promulgation and execution of his design is called the "servant of God." The prophets are called "servants of God" especially in this sense. (Amos 3:7; Haggai 2:23; Zec 1:6; Is 42:1–7; 49:1–6; 50:4–9; 52:13; 53:12; Jer 7:25; 1 Kgs 14:18; etc.)

---

[21]Josephus, *Anti.*, 8, 956.
[22]Hes., Frag., Pyndar, *Alymp.*, 2, 144; *Polit.*, 364C, 390E; Euripides, *Medea*, 964.

Paul accordingly addresses the "intellectuals" and denounces their cowardice in not fulfilling their prophetic mission to make public the judgment they had formed in their hearts against those degradations. "Therefore you have no excuse, oh man, whoever you are when you judge another, for in passing judgment upon him you condemn yourself" (Rom 2:1). The intellectual (the "gnostic") is aware of the immorality of the acts he observes around him and believes that that is enough. He has an individualistic conception of conscience. In 1 Cor 10:23-33 Paul inveighs against this reduction of conscience to *gnosis*. It is not enough to "know" that it is licit to eat meat that has been sacrificed to the idols. It is necessary besides to take into account the conscience of those who are not "gnostic," "of the weak in faith" (Rom 14:1). *Gnosis* is subject to charity.

In the present case Paul rebukes the pagan intellectuals for hiding the negative judgment, undoubtedly because of cowardice since a public denunciation of their vice-degraded religion would result in many and serious bad moments.

The internal logic of the sentences is clear. "Not only those who do such things deserve to die, but also those who approve them" (Rom 1:32). "Those who approve them" (*syneidokousin*) are the responsible intellectuals. And for that reason they "have no excuse" for they "judge" negatively "the other man," and in so doing "condemn themselves," since in virtue of this responsibility of denunciation, "in passing judgment upon them they condemn themselves, as if they were doing the very same things" (*ta gar auta prasseis o krinon*, Rom 2.1). In brief, the "gnostics," who in their hearts pass negative judgment on religious degradation, have an obligation to carry out a "prophetic" mission of denunciation. Otherwise they make themselves accomplices, guilty of the very faults they do not dare to denounce.

Paul now draws the conclusion: "if the judgment of God rightly falls upon those that do such things and make them their own (through cowardly omission) how will they escape the judgment of God?" (Rom 2:3).

In the following verses Paul continues to make special mention of the responsible intellectuals, who by their sin of omission "suppress the truth" (Rom 1:18). These, in fact, adopt a conscious attitude of despising the "kindness, patience, and forebearance of God" (2:4), having the same "hard and impertinent heart" (2:5).

This last expression reflects the atmosphere of the Exodus narrative in reference to Pharaoh's conscious resistance to the many divine signs which he even acknowledged (Ex 4:21; 7:8; 9:12; 14:4, 7).[23] Summing it up, the frustrated "pagan prophets" are the "children of rebellion and disobedient to truth to which they turn their backs in order to do evil" (Rom: 2:8).

Paul directs his main attacks against those responsible, those who are conscious of the degradation, those who suppress the expression of the truth they possess intellectually but which they do not want to translate into their lives, let alone boldly proclaim in every quarter.

He does not at all attempt to impose on their responsibility all the richness of "revealed" morality. It is enough to accuse them of inconsistence. "Those who have sinned without the law will also perish without the law" (Rom 2:12). "They certainly even though they do not have the law, do by nature what the law requires" (Rom 2:14). Or "their conscience also bears witness and their conflicting thoughts accuse or perhaps excuse them" (Rom 2:15). But they cowardly hide that light of truth not daring either to realize it in their own existence or to communicate it to others who are perhaps fatally enveloped in darkness. However, this situation of "truth suppression" will be unmasked "on that day when according to my gospel, God will judge the secrets of men by Christ Jesus" (Rom 2:16).

This is the great and vigorous denunciation that Paul directs to the pagan religious world. He refers mainly to the thinkers, to the more conscious individuals. Among them there was in fact a knowledge and recognition of God who appeared to them as a savior (*dynamis*) of their weakness and a lord (*theiotes*) of their finiteness. This presence of God was degraded in the most gross manner. God was made a god. His transcendence was sacrilegiously suppressed to make it fit the narrow patterns of human insufficiency. With it they had practically started the death of God.

Paul does not presume to condemn each individual of that society. He assails the sinful structure and those responsible for it. These were the people who still possessed a capacity for discernment and in fact condemned the situation in their hearts while

[23]In the same letter to the Romans Paul uses this expression in this sense, taking it from the Exodus context. Rom 9:18.

not daring to denounce it because of cowardice. They did not fulfill their prophetic mission but on the contrary suppressed the truth.

This shows that, for the apostle, pagan religiosity was valid and could be considered as a useful and necessary transition to the fulness of gospel proclamation. "Natural man" could undertake this imperfect and zigzagging course toward God. In his society there were some people responsible for the darkening of this way. For them there will be severe punishment on the day of discovery of the divine judgment.

Moral corruption can be avoided by human nature. It is the offspring of a positive sin committed by some responsible people and later on spread to the masses. Even outside the gospel there can be a valid moral purification whose direction is up to the "gnostics," the possessors of that "cognoscible" truth, the innate prophets of the "natural" world. As soon as these prophets cease to fulfill their mission of proclaiming the truth and denouncing its degradation, God is stripped of his transcendence in order to be incorporated into the circle of contingency, becoming a single piece (even though the principal one) of the tempo of human and worldly life.

They have just taken the first step toward atheism, an atheism which will be denounced by chosen spirits to whom the image of a useless and degraded God becomes repugnant.

Once Paul has described the religious situation of the pagan world, admitting its fundamental validity and pointing out those who are guilty of degrading it, he turns to the Jewish religious world and makes a deep analysis of the Hebrew religious society (Rom 2:17 to 3:31).

In the "natural" world there was a manifestation of God (conceived by pure human reflection) which imposed a noble and sufficient code of ethics. The true nature of the degradation was not a moral corruption which still kept the purity of the "gnosis," but the attempt to control the same "gnosis," changing the theology of the transcendent into a justifying theodicy of gross behavior. Paul condemns the intellectuals who were responsible for this degradation in that out of cowardice they did not struggle against it, thereby committing a grave sin of omission.

In Israel, on the contrary, the theology of the transcendent remained intact. This people possessed a "positive" manifestation of

God, which had even been codified and condensed in the sacred book. It was practically impossible to attempt a degradation of the revealed theology.

Furthermore, the possession of this "gnostic" superiority had become a reason for national pride. Certainly this positive revelation was entrusted to the Jews as an apostolic task of universal diffusion (Is 49:6; 54:1–3; 60:16; Tob 13:3–4; etc.). A Jew had the right to consider himself "a corrector of the foolish, guide to the blind, a light to those who are in darkness, a teacher of the children" (Rom 2:19–20). This is precisely the starting point for the apostle's denunciation: the Jews possessed this superior "gnosis," this "theology of the transcendent" and "boasted of it" (Rom 2:17). They regarded it as their own possession. This, in a sense, is considered as something positive, but Paul goes on with his sharp and piercing analysis. The possession of the gnosis of God imposes on the Jews a heavy burden: the task of communicating this gnosis to all the other men, and especially to the non-Jews.

This communication, however, could not be effected through a strictly gnostic method. It needed the channel of "testimony." Israel considered itself to have acquired its specific character by the possession of the law and revelation. The Israelites were the people of the law. As such they presented themselves to the exterior world, claiming for themselves gnostic superiority with respect to the divine message. However, this boasted possession of revelation was at times accompanied by immoral behavior. That, according to Paul, made impossible the acceptance of the message by outsiders. At the same time, the message cannot enter the human mind through a purely gnostic channel, despite its intrinsic greatness and its innate splendor of truth. The negative behavior of the official possessor of the message is like a dark body that hinders the flow of light through it.

Paul faces these "official teachers" of revelation, rebuking them for their ethical inconsistency. "And you who teach others, will you not teach yourself? You who preach against stealing, do you steal? You who say that one should not commit adultery, do you commit adultery? You who abhor idols, do you rob temples?" (2:21–22). Briefly, the Jew "boasting in the law dishonors God by breaking the law" (2:23). This glory taken from God is precisely the negative attitude of the outsiders when they discover the incongruities of the official possessors of revelation. "For the name of God is blasphemed among the Gentiles because of you" (Rom 2:24).

Paul then describes a society which possesses an authentic religious tradition but has converted religion into a purely sociological form of living together. The psychological traits of this hypocritical society are finally described by the apostle. The revealed message has remained intact. The theology has been enshrined in a very valuable reliquary, to which pure incense is offered. Membership in this religion develops into a bureaucracy on the national level. That, for example, was what happened to circumcision when the rite was reduced to a joining of the glorious people of the law. The apostle does not at all mean to say that the Israelite society had fallen in its totality into this state. He attempts, as in the case of the pagans, to describe the religious degradation in each one of these worlds. In Israel the hole through which the transcendent moves toward immanentization is not precisely the *gnosis* that is recognized intact and orally acknowledged as integral, but the terrible schizophrenia that disengages the *gnosis* from the *praxis*.

The *gnosis* thus isolated becomes byzantine and hardens. The whole pharisaic casuistry so strongly denounced (especially in the first gospel) is the best example of this divorce between doctrine and action. "The scribes and pharisees sat in Moses' seat, so practice whatever they tell you, but do not what they do. For they preach, but do not practice" (Mt 23:2–3). Jesus casts terrible anathemas on those "opportunists" of the Kingdom of God, whose doors "are shut before them, for they neither enter themselves, nor allow those that would enter, to go in" (Mt 23:13).

"For that reason," concludes Jesus, "I have decided to send prophets, and wise men, and scribes" (Mt 23:34). The solution was not to suppress the "scribe" but to convert him to what he should have been all along: a prophet. The byzantine scribe achieved equilibrium and stability through a shameful compromise between the intellectual oral acceptance of the message, and an evasive casuistry that in fact allowed a double life.

The new "scribe" (Mt 13:52) will carry upon his shoulders the whole risk of the prophetic mission. He will even be the victim of the purely "gnostic" scribes who will not tolerate a courageous denunciation of their hypocritical cynicism: "Many of them you will kill and crucify and will scourge in your synagogues and will persecute from town to town" (Mt 23:34).

As we see, long before Dostoyevsky in his novel *The Brothers Karamazov*, the first gospel had already sketched, in the worshipping assembly of the primitive Christian community, the sinister silhouette of the Grand Inquisitor.

Paul himself was vividly aware of the hazards of this prophetic mission which was essentially alien to his condition of being a Christian scribe. After having boldly affirmed his "deep understanding of the mystery of Christ" (Eph 3:4), that is, his high quality of Christian "scribe," he shudders to think of a possible byzantine isolationism: "for that reason I pray not to falter in the tribulations I suffer for your sake" (Eph 3:13). For Paul the "prophetic mission" of the scribe is intrinsically bound up with countless apostolic risks which have a constructive capacity for the Kingdom of God (Col 1:24; 2 Cor 4:10; 1 Cor 15:30; 2 Cor 11:23, etc.).

Summing it up, Paul denounces equally the responsible people in both religious worlds. Both were undoubtedly "intellectuals"— philosophers or scribes. This intellectual quality is a necessary requirement but it cannot exist in isolation or in separation from the prophetic mission. The "gnosis" of God cannot be possessed antiseptically, that is, without responsibility, which is often included as a consequence of a painful praxis.

The pagan intellectuals "suppressed truth as an authentic gesture of wickedness" hiding behind their silent and solitary judgment regarding the degradation of religion and lacking the courage to come out boldly with a denunciation that would involve them in risk.

The Jewish scribes admittedly continued to teach orally the revealed truth, but they presented it surrounded by the barbed wire of a casuistry which consisted in the last analysis in disengaging the praxis from the message. In a word, in both worlds the presence of God was beginning to grow cold because of the absence of the prophetic heat. The God of such intellectuals and "de-prophetized" scribes was agonizing slowly in those societies, in which religion had become a purely sociological form of living together.

And when in those worlds they persecuted and killed all their prophets, they actually decreed the proximate death of God.

PART II

RELIGIOUS MAN:

RESPONSIBLE

FOR HISTORY

CHAPTER 4

THE BIBLICAL MYSTIQUE IS NOT A MYSTIQUE OF ESCAPE, BUT OF COMMITMENT

What first attracts the attention of the historian of religion as he reads the Bible carefully is the identification of man's religious task and his creative commitment. In the Genesis narrative, creation ends only when God creates man who then becomes the creator's partner. Before man was created, God personally gave a name to every thing. "And God called light day, and darkness night. And God called the firmament heaven, and God called the dry land earth, and the waters that were gathered together he called seas" (Gen 1:5, 8, 10). We know what the name meant for the Semites. To "name" something was equivalent to having control over it. In this connection we must further observe that God names only things that are not within reach of man, but which form what might be called his objective environment: light, darkness, dry lands, waters. But he makes man the master of the fishes, the birds, and the animals, and that explains why the sacred author does not attribute to God the act of naming them. Once man was created, Yahweh "brought every beast of the field and every bird of the air, to the man to see what he would call them. And whatever the man called every living creature that was its name" (Gen 2:19). It must be remarked in this marvelous biblical mythology that God had not made any previous decision but had remained in expectation for the novelty of human action: "To see what he would call them." There is no previous planning of God that would curtail man's creative spontaneity.

Thus we understand why the divine element which makes man

like to God—his essentially religious quality—consists precisely in this autonomous and creative power with respect to evolution and to the ascending life of the historical cosmos. "And God said 'let us make man in our image, after our likeness and let him have dominion over the birds, the fish of the sea, and over the cattle, and over all the earth, and over every creeping thing that creeps upon the earth'" (Gen 1:26).

For this same reason man's creation is placed in the evening of the sixth day. Right afterwards it is said that "God rested from all his works that he had done" (Gen 2:2). Here for the first time in the history of religions a creative God adopts paradoxically a "hands-off" attitude so as not to interfere in the creative autonomy of his creature. The conclusion is clear. Prometheus is precisely the religious man of the Bible, the man who fulfills his religious task in the name and in the presence of a God who leaves him the freedom to decide for himself.

A fundamental fact in the whole biblical history, one that constitutes a symbol of the great salvation event (the resurrection of Christ), is the liberation of the Israelites from the yoke of Egyptian slavery.

What, then, is this slavery all about? It is simply what we could call, in modern times, "work alienation." Let us read the wonderful text of Exodus which relates and describes this great alienation from which God wants to free his people: "And Pharaoh said to his people: 'Behold, the people of Israel are too many and too mighty for us. Come, let us deal shrewdly with them, lest they multiply, and, if war befall us, they join our enemies and fight against us and escape from the land.' Therefore they set taskmasters over them to afflict them with heavy burdens; and they built for Pharaoh store-cities, Pithom and Raamses. But the more they were oppressed, the more they multiplied and the more they spread abroad. And the Egyptians were in dread of the people of Israel. So they made the people of Israel serve with rigor, and made their lives bitter with hard service, in mortar and brick, and in all kinds of work in the field; in all their work they made them serve with rigor" (Ex 1:9–14).

Here we have a magnificent description of work alienation. A privileged group becomes the master of the economy in a given region and utilizes the masses of the people as working instruments.

But in order to make the people function as instruments, it is necessary to make their work utterly exhausting, thereby preventing a normal development of their personality. Here we find ourselves very far away from the concept of work we have analyzed in the first pages of Genesis where God leaves the reins of creation, so to speak, in the hands of man, whom he makes his successor. Work according to the divine plan is a task that ennobles man and makes him the king of creation.

In Egypt, on the contrary, work had been deprived of its original dignity. The "lords" degraded work by taking it over. They pretended to occupy—sacrilegiously—the place of the creator and wanted to impose on others a task in which all tribes of Israel had to participate. Israel was a threat to the bourgeois security of the capitalist trust that exploited the vast riches of the Nile valley.

Work had become the most ignominious human alienation, precisely because it was an obstacle to personality expansion. What does God think of this oppressive condition of alienating labor into which his people have fallen? Are the priests and the prophets going to preach a doctrine of passive resignation, proposing as the final goal the happiness of heaven in some afterlife? Will they, at the sound of the trumpet, proclaim in the name of the Lord an eschatological reward for those who accept with resignation those terrible injustices? By no means. God has found his prophet, Moses, an Israelite by birth though a member of the aristocratic world of Pharaoh's household. God commands him to carry out an authentic process of "redemption by incarnation." Moses abandons the royal palace and rediscovers his proletarian people, in whose midst he had been born.

God said to Moses: "I have heard the groaning of the people of Israel whom the Egyptians hold in bondage and I have remembered my covenant. Say therefore to the people of Israel, 'I am the Lord, and I will bring you out from under the burdens of the Egyptians, and I will deliver you from their bondage, and I will redeem you with outstretched arm and with great acts of judgment, and I will take you for my people, and I will be your God. And you shall know that I am the Lord your God, who has brought you out from under the burdens of the Egyptians. And I will bring you into the land which I swore to give to Abraham, to Isaac, and to Jacob. I will give it to you for a possession. I am the Lord" (Ex 6:5–8).

This sense of immediate liberation of the people of Israel was also grasped by the authors of the New Testament who never yielded to the temptation of transferring the history of Exodus to an after life. Thus the author of the Epistle to the Hebrews comments on the events we have just mentioned: "By faith Moses, when he was born, was hid for three months by his parents, because they saw that the child was beautiful; and they were not afraid of the king's edict. By faith Moses, when he was grown up, refused to be called the son of Pharaoh's daughter, choosing rather to share ill-treatment with the people of God than to enjoy the fleeting pleasures of sin" (Heb 11:23–25).

This mystique of commitment goes on throughout the sacred legislation as it is contained in the three books of the Pentateuch: Exodus, Leviticus, and Deuteronomy. According to this view the new life of Israel was modeled on a type of "religious socialism," totally dedicated to preventing the accumulation and concentration of possessions and the resulting danger for the people of returning to a proletarian condition. It is really marvelous to observe how the great divine adventure that permeates the whole Bible refers to an evident design on the part of God to liberate his people from this miserable proletarian condition in order to bring them to a decidedly "socialized" situation, one in which conception of the means of production as a "right of use and abuse" becomes impossible.

Naturally the specific Hebrew legislation is impractical today, for our circumstances are totally different. But the Bible shows that a religious view of society cannot avoid these problems. It must, on the contrary, project itself into them, thereby implying an attitude of commitment and even of risk. It is impossible to go through the whole Bible here in order to see every single evidence of this mystique of commitment. Suffice it simply to refer to what I would call "prophetic realism." The prophets, the religious leaders of the people, were decidedly not escapees from reality, men who cared only about "spiritual things" in the hellenistic sense of the word. On the contrary, they were marvelously informed about the political and social situation of their people. They spoke a concrete, direct, and even dangerous language. Ezekiel rebukes some "foolish prophets" for "following their own spirit without seeing anything" (Ez 13:3).

Coming to the New Testament we find there a whole mystique

of commitment, especially in the pauline epistles. Paul's insistence on the eschatological resurrection offers the foundation of a mystique of attachment to matter. There is a whole theology of the body and the world in his letters.

There were some "greek" Christians in Corinth who would repeat the old epicurean slogans: "Food is meant for the stomach, and the stomach is meant for food" (1 Cor 6:13). That is, the life of the body is temporal. The dialectic "food and stomach" is temporary and God himself will bring an end to it. It is a typically Greek conception. The interesting thing is the spirit that never dies. The body is something provisional and futile. Thus lust and other excesses cannot soil the spirit, the only heir of God's judgment. Paul's answer is clear: "The body is not meant for immorality, but for the Lord, and the Lord for the body. And God who raised the Lord will also raise us up by his power" (1 Cor 6:13–14). In his answer Paul places faith in the resurrection of the body as the central element in his moral argumentation. Body is defined by a religious relationship with the Lord. The risen Christ, the redeemer, has an active relationship with the body. It is not something temporary and transient. On the contrary, the body will be raised as a consequence of Christ's resurrection. Briefly, there is a sexual morality in Christianity because of the eschatological importance given to the body.

But it is precisely from the point of view of eschatology that Christianity has been charged with the mystique of escape or evasion. To be honest, we can never forget that Christianity is essentially eschatological. Paul in his first letter to the Thessalonians describes the essence of the Christian attitude: "To serve a living and true God, and to wait for his Son from heaven whom he raised from the dead, Jesus, who will deliver us from the wrath to come" (1 Thes 1:9–10).

From the eschatological angle Marxist humanism has assailed the Christian mystique and morality in two respects: (1) Christianity makes the human task relative. Work is reduced to a purely moral eschatology of merit totally related to the acquisition of an eschatological reward, utterly unrelated to what is achieved by the earthly effort. (2) Since human hope is completely directed to the acquisition of a reward beyond history, everything else is considered as provisional, transient, and temporary.

But Paul himself grasped perfectly the danger of this misunderstanding. Indeed in the same letter to the Christian community of Thessalonica, he explained that the Christian's eschatological expectation runs the risk of weakening the intrinsic validity of human work: "We exhort you, brethren, to do so more and more, and to aspire to live quietly. To mind your own affairs, and to work with your hands, as we charged you. So that you may command the respect of outsiders and be dependent on nobody" (1 Thes 4:10–12). This shows that "eschatological evasionism" was already a sin of the first Christian communities and that outsiders had started to criticise religious alienation insofar as it was in opposition to the human value of work. Paul's reaction is unmistakable. It even seems somewhat violent; we can understand why Paul himself renounces his own apostolic right of living at the expense of the community of believers, in order to avoid any misunderstanding in this respect. "Remember, brethren, our labor and toil. We worked night and day that we might not burden any of you while we preached to you the gospel of God" (1 Thes 2:9). Reading Paul carefully we discover that the eschatological character of Christianity is not related to a pre-existing reality like a coveted prize, that would be the goal in the final victory. To make the Christian position unambiguous, we should talk of "eschatologization" rather than of "eschatology."

This eschatologizing tempo of human history is described by Paul very well in Chapter eight of his letter to the Romans: "for creation waits with eager longing for the revealing of the sons of God. We know that the whole creation has been groaning in labor until now" (Rom 8:19, 22).

The real sin that we westerners have committed against the Biblical message, basing our views on the classical philosophy of evasion and pure spirit, consists in the introduction of a dichotomy between the "here and now" and the "thereafter." By doing this we have split apart what God created one and indivisible.

The second criticism levelled against Christian morality is that it is a morality of good intention. A historian of Christian spirituality would have his work cut out in describing the many deviations through which the biblical message has been corrupted throughout history. In this sense, the biblical revival offers us some extraordinary surprises. Suffice it to quote here one important pauline text. Writing to the Corinthians, Paul exhorts the faithful to overcome sectarianism and to build the kingdom of God in an efficient manner. "According to the commission of God given to me, like a skilled master builder I laid a foundation, and another man is building upon it. Let each man take care how he builds upon it. For no other foundation can any one lay than that which is laid, which is Jesus Christ. Now if any one builds on the foundation with gold, silver, precious stones, wood, hay, or stubble, each man's work will become manifest; for the day will disclose it, because it will be revealed with fire, and the fire will test what sort of work each man has done. If the work which any man has built on the foundation survives, he will receive a reward. If any man's work is burned up, he will suffer loss, though he himself will be saved, but only as through fire" (1 Cor 3:10–15).

Here Paul shows the positive way in which Christians must fulfill the task of building a church. This task implies an "effort," a "work" (*kopos*, v.8). This effort must produce an objective result whose end will necessarily coincide with the finished work itself. The man of good faith who has made a mistake in his technique of construction will not be excluded from the kingdom of God, but the kingdom of God could not have been built up had there not been builders endowed with an objectively effective technique. That is why the kingdom of God, according to Paul, is closely connected with the intrinsic dynamics of the historical evolution of a world waiting for the *parousia*. That is why a mystique of a morality of good intentions alone is not enough for the effective eschatologization of human history. Paul himself, even though his conscience is clear, is always preoccupied with the objective efficiency of his apostolic work (cfr. Gal 2:2; 4:11).

Finally we can firmly assert that the biblical mystique and morality do not deter man from his task of "changing the world," but on the contrary, his religious condition as such impels him forcefully to an uncompromising cosmic and historical commitment.

CHAPTER 5

The Biblical Mystique of Commitment Is Gratuitous

It is necessary to go a little deeper into the "religious" meaning of the Christian's temporal commitment, for otherwise we run the risk of falling into what we could call the "inflation of grace."

Indeed we believers, Christians especially, have exploited for too long the great emptiness that God's death has left in the atheistic conscience, taking advantage of the great aspiration to fill it which we knew would arise. We attempt to dialogue with those who do not believe, starting with a *datum* we assume is common to both, namely man's intrinsic need for total fulfillment. But lo and behold, the atheists tell us sincerely that they do not believe in any of that. "Absolutely nothing," says one of them. "I have, on the contrary, a sense of a full internal universe, full as a solid and self-sufficient egg."[1]

The same writer observes that even in terms of moral standards God marks the difference between the two kinds of human behavior. "If God were," he writes, "as important as you think he is, to believe in him or not should produce almost two human races, as it were, with irreconcilable rules of life. We see clearly that nothing of the sort happens. Fear of hell keeps us from sin as much as fear of capital punishment keeps us from murder. With or without faith there are kind and wicked people, compassionate and cruel, heroes and saints and even wise men; the presence or absence of faith

[1]Roger Ikor, *Dieu aujourd'hui*, Paris, 1965, p. 50.

barely changes the mental scenery of man."[2] And he concludes: "Let me put it a little crudely: God is good for nothing."

Here is an affirmation that seems sacrilegious yet nevertheless constitutes an exact formulation of the purest biblical theology. The biblical God is a luxury. He is completely gratuitous. God is a grace. Fr. Henri de Lubac in his recent book *The Mystery of the Supernatural* makes a very important observation, one capable of breaking this impasse that the dialogue between Christians and unbelievers has reached. Historically, he says, Catholic theology used the hypothesis of "pure nature" for experimental purposes, only to allow this hypothetical reality to infiltrate later into the theological set-up, thereby creating tremendous confusion. He blames the current difficulty in dialogue with atheists on that confusion.

The Christian does indeed believe that historical man, the only one who actually exists, is intrinsically destined for God. The end and success of the human adventure is an eternal embrace with God. But this "destiny" is totally gratuitous. In human reality, even in its actual historical condition, there is no necessity for God at all. De Lubac gave a correct interpretation to St. Thomas' expression according to which the wish to see God is a *desiderium naturae*, when he wrote as follows: "This expression which St. Thomas uses on several occasions, should be enough in itself to do away with any tendency to fancy interpretation. It therefore remains necessary to show how, even for a being animated with such a desire, there still is not and cannot be any question of such an end being 'owed' —in the sense in which the word rightly gives offense. It remains to show how it is always by grace—even apart from the traditional question of sin and its forgiveness—that God 'shows himself to him.' "[3]

In the first three chapters of his letter to the Romans, Paul admits that God, the God of Abraham, Isaac, and Jacob, was present to the pagan world. And he explicitly calls this divine presence in the world a "revelation" and "a faith" (Rom 1:17, 19).

[2] R. Ikor, *op. cit.*, p. 51.

[3] H. de Lubac, *The Mystery of the Supernatural*, Herder and Herder, New York, 1967, p. 75–6. De Lubac quotes St. Thomas in *Contra Gentiles*, I, 3, c. 52.

The gospel, for Paul, is nothing but a "fulness" and "a revelation" (*apokalypsis*) of a manifestation of God which was in a sense implicit.

This means that, according to Christian faith, in fact (in the historical reality of this concrete humanity) God is not required by human nature. He is a pure gift, a pure grace. The encounter of man with God necessarily takes place through faith. In the New Testament, especially in Paul, two stages can be distinguished—dialectically combined—of this faith. A general or universal level encompasses all men of good faith who have not rejected consciously and culpably the "green light" of positive revelation. The second, more restricted level includes those who, after having discerned this light, have accepted it consciously and act accordingly in their personal life and their social expansion

Among the first we find the atheists. The atheist of "good faith" for us lives and acts enwrapped in grace, but for mysterious reasons which we cannot grasp he has not arrived at the explicit knowledge of this God and of this grace that enwraps him and constitutes the unknown end of his road.

If we start from the great principle of God's gratuity, we believers cannot demand from our partner in dialogue that he recognize that the religious dimension of man forms a great part of human fulness. In good logic the atheistic dialogue partner has the right to exclude God and religion from his *Weltanschauung* because by hypothesis he has not yet perceived consciously God's gratuitous presence in history.

Specifically, the fact that atheists are happy with an intrahistorical transcendence is perfectly logical and for us believers does not imply an alienating attitude. The scholastic theologians have also recognized this legitimacy of the "atheistic" position. John of St. Thomas writes: "Man by nature does not have an ultimate end materially determined and particular, but only vaguely and in common and under the aspect of happiness and beatitude."[4] In short, in a dialogue with atheists, Christians are supposed by their own faith not to demand (outside the framework of faith) the recognition of the divine or religious element as a component of human fulfillment.

If, in consequence, we believers cannot honestly charge the atheist

[4]John of St. Thomas, *Cursus Theologicus*, disp. 12, Numb. 23.

with being illogical because he asserts a human progress without God, will the atheists then, by the same token, have the right to accuse us of alienation because we have made God the ultimate end of human aspirations?

In fact R. Garaudy recognizes that "the greatness of religion is proven by the exigency of answering these questions; its weakness and its defectiveness lie in pretending to give them a dogmatic answer, which must ever be bound up with a certain stage of knowledge, and which, while bearing the stigma of the transitory inadequacies of the age, is offered as definitive and even as sacred."[5]

In brief, in speaking of religious alienation it is necessary to agree with this fundamental objection if the answer of faith is demanded by a human question. And in this case we would not have avoided the difficulty of which we have just spoken. This "answer of faith" would be necessary for a human fulfillment and nature could not be conceived or developed without this element of divine origin. Such a solution would have affirmed again that God (grace) is demanded by nature.

More specifically a religious answer *demanded* by nature would be an unwanted rival of man's autonomy. Reading the Bible, we find almost everywhere this fundamental affirmation: grace is neither a key to the enigma of life, nor the rival of man's creative autonomy. Grace is not an intruder about to eclipse the epic grandeur of Prometheus.

We grant gladly that when a religious "response" is presented as the solution of intellectual enigmas or as an intrinsic link between intrahistoric dynamism and human evolution it becomes an alienating element that as such hinders the Promethean impulse of the human adventure. We also admit that at the very same moment such a "religious answer" has been totally degraded and has as a result lost its essential characteristic: its "gratuity."

Here we find the central point for a deep dialogue between the Christian and the atheist.

We Christians must ponder very carefully this need for the infinite, this kind of intrahistoric transcendence that constitutes the greatness of the *praxis* of atheistic humanism. Meanwhile, if we start from our Christian faith, we have no right to demand the

[5] R. Garaudy, *From Anathema to Dialogue*, Herder and Herder, New York, 1966, p. 89.

recognition of religion as an intrinsic component demanded by nature.

On the other hand, atheists must reconsider our theological affirmation of the gratuity of God and religion. This gratuity most definitely insures that the religious answer, from its very beginning, does not become a rival of human independence and that it does not hinder the freedom of movement of man's ascending evolution.

A dialogue of this kind would eliminate the possibility of a reciprocal anathema: the accusation of an "alienating danger."[6]

[6]E. Jacob, *Théologie de l'Ancien Testament*, Neuchâtel-Paris, 1955, pp. 160 ff.

CHAPTER 6

COSMIC CONTEXT OF HUMAN SALVATION

Man's evolution and destiny always appear in the Bible in a bond of total solidarity with the cosmic context within which he is located. The whole history of humanity is "sacral" because all mankind can and should be redeemed and saved. The announcement of salvation is general. The "history of salvation" does not begin with man's sin, nor even with his creation, but with the creation of the universe (cfr. Ps 135–136).[1]

The whole of the Old Testament is a linear history in progressive evolution in which God's intervention in the drama of successive events is presented in such a way as to give them a sense of maturation with regards to a future and total redemption. The sense of "expectation" that permeates all this historical process of maturation toward salvation is remarkable. History in the Old Testament is the most characteristic category through which human thought can be expressed. In the cultural heritage of the near East, in whose midst the Old Testament literature was born and developed, there were many myths of creation and consummation. But the Bible has historicized them. Babylonian and phoenician myths spoke of a primeval struggle between two opposing divinities. And even perhaps in some poetic texts of the Old Testament this myth shows up as a struggle of Yawheh as between two sea monsters, the successful result of which enables him to organize heaven and earth (Ps 74:12–17; 89:10–13; Is 51:9–10; Jos 26:10–12; 38:1–11; Ps 104:26). But faith in the God of history has made a historical

[1] S. Lyonnet, *Exegesis Epistulae ad Romanos*, Pontifical Biblical Institute, Rome, 1962, p. 80.

reality of Rahab: Egypt. Leviathan has become an animal that Yahweh has brought under complete control (Ps 104:26). The *"tihamat"* of Babylonian mythology has become the *"tehom,"* that is, the sea. The faith of Israel has been subjected to a radical "demythologization." What remains is the deep essence of myth, totally translated into the terms of history: God's direct intervention in the world.[2]

The divine sense of history is manifest, above all, through the prophets. The prophets are the most genuine representatives of the transcendence of the Most High and Absolute God of the rigorous Jewish monotheism. However, this prophetic intervention is not a-temporal or abstract but mingles thoroughly with the course of history in order to sustain an all-out struggle against the deviations of human freedom. The prophets do not summon their listeners to a mystique of escape or evasion. On the contrary, they urge the political institutions and their leaders to commit themselves in a given direction according to God's requirements. It is as if God needed to have history assume a fixed course, in order that his plans of salvation may be realized. The salvation unceasingly announced by the prophets is totally intrahistorical and presupposes the successive accumulation of human and worldly events.

The salvation announced by the prophets certainly aims at a final fulfillment, but it is being realized partially as history unfolds. The events follow each other in a progressive linear manner, moving in a zigzag course as a result of the introduction of evil, which was ultimately caused by man's and the angels' freedom.

The literary style itself with which the different stages of salvation are announced takes on a corporeal, terrestrial, and cosmic coloring. The process is, in consequence, diametrically opposed to a gnostic or manichean conception of redemption. Paul is fully aware of this sense of history maturing toward salvation, when after recalling the main events of Exodus he recognizes that "these things happened to them for a warning, but they were written down for our instruction upon whom the end of the ages has come" (1 Cor 10:11).

The appearance of Christ, likewise, even though due to a vertical intervention from the divine counsel, depends nevertheless on the same evolving course of history. "When the time had fully come

[2]E. Jacob, *Théologie de l'Ancien Testament*, Neuchâtel-Paris, 1955, pp. 160 ff.

God sent forth his son, born of woman, born under the law" (Gal 4:4). This whole view of "expectation," of dependence on the temporal progression of events, is rather common in Paul. In describing the different salvific phases of history, he employs various temporal expressions like "until . . .": "The law was added because of transgressions, *until* the offspring should come to whom the promise had been made" (Gal 3:19). "Now *before* faith came, we were confined under the law, kept under restraint *until* faith should be revealed" (Gal 3:23). "Therefore the law was our custodian *until* Christ came, that we may be justified by faith *at the end*" (Gal 3:24).

Even though Christ has *already* come and has achieved radical victory there is still a certain tension between the "already" and the "still." The Christian is *already* a son, but *still* an heir (Gal 4:5-7). Man's "divine sonship" will have to manifest itself in a climactic moment of history. The arrival of that moment cannot be hastened since it is dependent on the same vital evolution. For that reason, creation is still waiting for this completion of its becoming (Rom 8:19). Paul *does not know* how long it will take to go from the "now" of a salvation already begun to the final moment of maturation, but he is sure that there is an ascending progress of history between both terms.

"For as in Adam all died, so also in Christ shall all be made alive, but each in his own order: Christ, the first fruits, then at his coming those that belong to Christ. Then comes the end, when he delivers the kingdom to God the Father after destroying every rule, and every authority, and power" (1 Cor 15:22-24).

Between the resurrection of Christ as "first fruits" and the final event of the resurrection of those "that are Christ's" there must be an upward motion of history, all of it dominated by the varied details of a struggle between Christ and "the powers." This struggle is coextensive with the progressive evolution of the world. "For he must reign *until* he has put all his enemies under his feet" (1 Cor 15:25).

What this means is that Christ's action is like a "sustained effort" (which in the long run will succeed), all of it concentrated in "the last enemy to be destroyed, death" (1 Cor 15:26). It is very interesting to observe that in this Chapter 15 of the first letter to the Corinthians, where Paul insists so much on the order (the

"turning," *en tō ido tagmati,* 15:23) of the chronological succession
of salvation history, the whole coloring of the context is terrestrial and corporeal. It is fundamentally a matter of the eschatological
resurrection. Paul fails to find suitable expressions and metaphors
to convey the fully material meaning of the great final event of
human evolution in "Christ."

We can draw as a minimal conclusion from this brief excursion
into the historical perspective that deeply permeates the whole
Bible, the necessity of granting an intrinsic value to human effort
insofar as it is a progressive building toward ultimate fulfillment.
From the dawn of his existence man constantly strives for self-
advancement. This advancement encompasses different realms of
his existential possibilities, all of which are funneled into the unique
enterprise of self-improvement. The biblical concept of "man" is
decidedly integralist, contrary to any gnostic or manichean dichotomy.
Advancement must encompass the whole of human reality as we
find it *de facto* in human existence.

Especially for Paul salvation refers to human reality, which,
when connected with Christ, can achieve its fulfillment. When the
apostle describes positively the life of the adopted children of
God, he stresses the intimate relationship between filial adoption
and the reception of "the spirit of the son of God" (Gal 4:6–7;
Rom 8:15–16).

For Paul the word "spirit" has all the rich semitic nuances of
the Old Testament. The *"ruach"* was the wind, the breath, bearer
of life and power both in nature and in man. In the pauline texts
we are now considering, the "spirit" is some sort of *vital drive in
man toward his own conscious realization.* Thus in Rom. 8:16, the
divine "spirit" makes our "spirit" aware of the fact that we are
God's children. In 1 Cor 2:11 the "spirit of man recognizes what
is within himself." But the "spirit" entails not only this "awareness"
of its own being, but also the tendency to build itself up in a
given direction. "The tendency of the flesh is death, but the
tendency of the spirit is life and peace" (Rom 8:6).

Thus we can understand why Paul so seldom speaks of "spirit"
as a purely human effort of self-improvement (1 Cor 2:11–12;
Rom 8:15). In any case since the result of this effort is negative
("death" Rom 8:6; "the fear of the slave," Rom 8:15) it does
not deserve the name "spirit."

To sum up, this thrust toward resurrection that the presence of the spirit in man brings about is not conceived of by Paul as an escape or evasion from cosmic reality within whose framework the life of the "new man" takes place. The "spirit" makes man aware that he is "son of God" and therefore "heir." This "heritage" has God as its object and is realized on the same level as Christ's. "Coheirs with Christ." This "participation" in Christ's heritage clearly refers to the resurrection. "We will be glorified with him" but in order to achieve this fulfillment an effort must be made first, the same effort Christ made. "We suffer with him, we will also be glorified with him" (Rom 8:17).

This effort-toward-resurrection is made in close solidarity with the cosmos, which is in a sense dependent on the final success of mankind's "spiritual" effort, since its own destiny is bound to it (Rom 8:18–22).

The "righteous" man is bearer of the "Spirit." Far from being an alienation and separation from the world and its history, the Spirit constitutes the "first fruits," (Rom 8:23) of his definitive "redemption"—a redemption that clearly supposes not a negation, but a sublimation of matter (Rom 8:23, tēn apolytrōsin tou sōmatos hēmōn).

Therefore, according to Paul, the activity of "man-spirit" toward the fulfillment of his existence cannot be considered as something divorced from the normal evolution of the conscious human effort. The "spirit" does not descend upon man to tear him away from his natural habitat and transfer him to some ethereal place, but on the contrary, to help him along the intracosmic itinerary toward his own existential realization.

For that reason, pauline morality implies an immanence of the Christian's baptized effort in the same vital ascensional thrust of the human and worldly event. It is not reduced to waiting sluggishly for a "deus ex machina" to descend and force his violent way into the mystically relaxed and passive soul. On the contrary, it implies a constant activity, a continuous effort to conquer those "tendencies of the flesh."

In a form of humanism rather frequently found among Christian thinkers the biological evolution of man is simply a false front for his moral advancement under the influence of grace. In pauline humanism, just the opposite takes place. Human morality, even though ennobled by grace, would not have a positive value were it not intimately linked to a full biological success: the resurrection.

Indeed if there were no resurrection, "those also that had fallen asleep in Christ, would have perished" (1 Cor 15:18). "If for this life only we had hope in Christ, we are of all men to be pitied the most" (1 Cor 15:19). "If the dead are not raised at all, . . . why am I in peril every hour? What do I gain if, humanly speaking, I fought with beasts at Ephesus? If the dead are not raised, let us eat and drink for tomorrow we die" (1 Cor 15:30–32).

According to this biblical vision grace is not reduced to creating the possibility of a *moral* dimension of man. On the contrary, it penetrates all the meanderings of his existential make-up. "Sacral" humanism attempts to confine the first bursting forth of the kingdom of God to just one segment of human and world evolution, the moral one, as though it alone would—duly transformed—pass the frontiers of the kingdom. The result would be that all other manifestations of human culture would be perishable and provisional. They would be only a pedestal for the kingdom, a favorable climate, a removing of obstacles. But in the long run they would not be called to salvation and would inexorably die in the final conflagration.

It is obvious that human effort—work—has in this humanistic purview no sufficient justification. It is humiliated and degraded. In biblical humanism, on the contrary, human effort is *intrinsically* necessary, although not *sufficient*, to achieve total and complete fulfillment: resurrection. As long as humanity has not attained to an adequate level of maturity it will not be ready for resurrection. Without the influence of grace, human effort will not be able to achieve fulfillment. But grace does not take the place of this effort. It only strengthens it, radically heals it and sublimates it.

That is why grace radically abhors any "ghetto" seclusion. Grace has to get lost in the midst of things, among the efforts, deep in the stages of the progressive evolution of history.

CHAPTER 7

RELIGIOUS MAN AND HUMAN ALIENATION

Atheistic humanism, largely developed by Karl Marx, has grown into a massive problem of planetary dimensions. In what follows I will be referring primarily to the marxist presentation.

According to Marx, man is defined on the basis of his relationship to nature and to other men. The fact that an oligarchy has taken over the control of this nature and has kept the masses from self-determination constitutes the greatest degradation of human beings. Socialism has come to take away the control of nature from the hands of a few rulers and to return it to the masses. After all, only the masses will be able to carry out the humanization of the universe.

For Marx the fact that this ruling oligarchy has been able to maintain the monopoly of human development is due ultimately to the mighty power of the myth of a creative God. This view of things is already found in the works of the young Marx, as is evident in the *Manuscripts of 1844:* "A being is considered autonomous (*selbstständig*) only when he is his own master. And he is not his own master except when he owes his own existence to himself. A man that lives thanks to somebody else is considered a dependent being. But I live entirely thanks to another being not only if I owe him the preservation of my life, but also if *he has created my life*, if he is its origin," if it is not my own creation.

Marxist atheism is affirmed on the basis of this "socialist" conception of history and of man. The elimination of an outside creator is not postulated by abstract reasoning, but results necessarily from the socialist *praxis*, since man's deep reality excludes the reality of God.

The death of God is a condition previous to and concomitant with man's salvation through his own progressive realization in history. "Since for the socialist man *the whole so-called universal history* is nothing but the procreation of man through human work, that is, the evolution of nature for man, this same socialist man has the evident and irrefutable proof of his self-creation, of the process *of his birth.*"

"From the very moment that the *essentiality (wesenhaftigkeit)* of man and nature became practically visible to man in his real human condition, the question relative to an *alien (fremd)* being, to a being placed above nature and man (a question that involves the admission of the non-essentiality [*Unwesentlichkeit*] of nature and man), has become for all practical purposes an impossible question."

In order to understand properly the atheism of Marx and of all his followers, it is essential to keep in mind constantly that the death of God is basically demanded by the strength of the socialist *praxis.* Man's essentiality, that is, his progressive self-creation through work in the midst of an ascending history, does not allow the intrusion of an outsider who would deprive him of this total responsibility.

A superficial reading of Marx, however, could give the idea that for the great philosopher the notion of "religious alienation" occupies a primordial place in the purifying function of socialist *praxis.* Just the opposite. For Marx religious alienation is a consequence and expression of political alienation. He presents this idea in a lucid and poetic manner in his *Introduction to the Critique of Hegel's Philosophy of Law.* The point he makes is that the wretched man living in a bourgeois society dreams up a transcendent universe as a way to justify his own situation.

"Man is no abstract being squatting outside the world. Man is the *world* of man, the state, society. This state and society produce religion, which is a kind of reversed world-consciousness, because they are a *reversed world.* Religion is the general theory of that world, its encyclopaedic compendium, its logic in a popular form, its spiritualist *point d'honneur,* its enthusiasm, its moral sanction, its solemn completion, its universal ground for consolation and justification. It is the *fantastic realization* of the human essence because the *human essence* has no true reality. The struggle against religion is therefore mediately the fight against *the other world,* of which religion is the spiritual *aroma*."[1] This is why the socialist *praxis*, even though *chronologically* it begins its critique "by unmasking the aspect of holiness of human alienation," has as its primary purpose to "unmask alienation in its unholy aspects." And thus, Marx concludes, "the critique of heaven turns into the critique of the earth, the critique of religion into the critique of law, and the critique of theology into the critique of politics."[2]

The opium of the people

From this strict perspective of the demands of socialist *praxis*, we can understand the famous phrase, made popular by Marx, that "religion is the opium of the people."[3]

Marx does not say that religion is an opium *for* the people, but the opium *of* the people, *Das Opium des Volks*. He does not believe, with the philosophers of the Enlightenment, that religion was created by a class of profiteers and clergy. Religion is the narcotic of the people. It is the people who themselves take this sedative in order to bear their misery. Religion, segregated by misfortune, carries hope, and men need hope. But this hope is false. And this religious evasion hinders human development in such a way that, according to Lenin, it is impossible to undertake an effective struggle in favor of a higher order without first destroying religious sentiment. This contention on the lips of Lenin assumes the form of an efficient, demagogic, and antitheistic proclamation: "The weakness of the exploited classes in their struggles against the exploiters inevitably generates a belief in a better after life, in the same manner that the weakness of the savage in the struggles against nature generates a belief in the gods, the devils and miracles. Religion preaches humility and resignation in this world to those who spend their whole life in travail and misery, consoling them with the hope of a heavenly reward. On

---

[1] K. Marx, *Contribution to the Critique of Hegel's Philosophy of Right*. Reprinted by permission of Schocken Books Inc. from *On Religion*, by K. Marx and Fried. Engels, Shocken Books, 1964, p. 41.

[2] K. Marx, *op. cit.*, p. 42.

[3] It was not Karl Marx, as is well known, who first compared religion with opium. In 1838 Feuerbach had already used this comparison, and later on it was also employed by H. Heine, B. Bauer, Proudhon and Goethe. Cfr. M. Reding, *Der politische Atheismus*, 1958, p. 123.

the other hand, religion teaches those who earn their living by the
work of others to be generous in this world, thus offering an
easy justification of their existence as exploiters and giving them a
cheap ticket to the joys of heaven. Religion is the opium of the
people. Religion is a kind of spiritual vodka in which the slaves
of capitalism drown their human personality and their claim to
a life worthy of human beings. But the slave who has achieved
an awareness that he can gain freedom is already half way to
freedom. The conscientious modern worker, educated by organized
industry and instructed by city life, disdainfully rejects religious
prejudices. He leaves heaven to be manipulated by the clergy
and by bourgeois religious society, building for himself a better life
on this earth. The modern proletarian sides with socialism, which
enlists science in the struggle against the darkness of religion and
liberates the worker from the belief in an after life. Socialism
organizes the proletarians in an effective campaign to achieve a
better life on earth."

The study of Christianity as "alienating" has to proceed on
two superimposed levels. The first level is that of historical realization, and here a conscientious and responsible Catholic must admit
the concrete forms in which the message of Christ has been
used as a brake on human development. The formidable self-criti-
cism carried out so freely during Vatican Council II testifies to the
willingness of the Catholic Church to admit her guilt in this matter.

But on a second level, the Catholic theologian must bring the
problem to the realm of the ideal. And to do so he must make a
study of the Christian message and find out if man's religious
dimension, as presented by the Christian, is truly alienating in
the sense criticized by Marx.

The Bible and religious alienation

Naturally, this theological reflection must be carried out, just
as any other, in the light of the Bible. Christianity is a religion
of the "Book" and its full justification has to be made always
with regard to the "Book."

Throughout the whole Bible, the religious dimension of man
is presented in intimate and close relation with his human temporal
development. He is presented in Genesis as God's image. To be

the image of God is something that refers to what today, as we have already said, we call man's religious dimension. In a word, Man is presented as the image of God precisely because to him is entrusted the task of carrying out the completion of the work of Creation. "Then God said, let us make man in our image, after our likeness, let him have dominion over the fish of the sea, and over the birds of the air, and over the cattle, and over all the earth, and over every creeping thing that creeps upon the earth" (Gen 1:26). In other religions, this "religious element" is given as an alternative to the human and worldly task of man. To be "connected" with God he must renounce or lessen the task of human and worldly construction. In biblical religion, on the contrary, the intrinsic religious dimension of man consists precisely in his responsibility over this construction of himself and the world. Man is God's likeness—he is linked to him—because he is going to bring to fulfillment the task of creation begun by God.

This "religious" task of worldly construction is intimately connected with the material and corporeal dimension of the human and earthly being. The hope in an eschatological resurrection of the body cannot be understood except by presupposing the intrinsic religious validity of matter itself. Christian faith, centered in Christ's and man's resurrection, allows us to assert, strange as it may seem to some, that our religion is essentially "materialistic." Matter and time are taken extremely seriously throughout the whole Bible.

Christian morality is also directed primarily toward man rather than toward God. The first and main precept is the love of neighbor. God is always sought through the brother. Faith is a dialogue between man and God, in which the latter accosts man with this insistent question: "Where is your brother?" (Gen 4:9). In Chapter 25 of Matthew's gospel God is so completely represented by the neighbor, that even the "righteous" have failed to discover the exact relation between neighbor and God. Hence their surprised question: "Lord, when did we see you hungry, and thirsty, and naked, and in prison?" The purest Christian theology, therefore, does not admit the possibility of a religious alienation but rejects it completely. When we are faced with a concrete instance of religion being conceived of or used as a brake on human progress, we can be certain that this is not the religion which inspired the whole of the literary riches of the Bible. Treason has been committed against the pure essence of biblical teaching about man.

Religion and human fulfillment in marxism

Starting from this base we can formulate a new question. Can marxist philosophy validly eliminate the possibility of religion, not as an alienation, but as a dynamic perfection of human development?

"Throughout the series of alienations and of the struggles to overcome them, need becomes properly speaking *human*, that is to say, *social*. And once man is made totally real by overcoming his alienation, the needs that he will have satisfied will not only be the biological necessities that first goaded him on: hunger and rebellion against pain, but also the needs of the totality of human life."[4] Therefore, why make the *a priori* denial that the totality of human life also includes the development of humanness?

Erich Fromm, in a very interesting study on *Marx and his concept of man*, makes this important observation: "The whole concept of alienation was first expressed in western thought, in the concept of idolatry in the Old Testament. The essence of what the prophets call idolatry is not that man adores many gods instead of one. It is the fact that the idols are man's handiwork—they are things—and man kneels and adores things: he adores what he himself has created. In so doing, he becomes a thing. He transfers to things of his own creation the attributes of his own life, and instead of acknowledging himself as a creative person, he is in contact with himself only through the worship of an idol. He has become an alien to his own vital forces, to the richness of his own potentialities, and is in contact with himself only indirectly, as in submission to the frozen life of the idols."

Fromm a little later, speaking as a psychiatrist, dares to give a diagnosis of this human quality. "Actually, this is also the psychology of a fanatic. He is empty, dead, and deprived, but in order to compensate for the state of depression and interior death he chooses an idol, be it the state, or the party, or an idea, or the Church, or God. He makes this idol an absolute and subjects himself to

[4]R. Garaudy, *Perspectives de l'Homme*, Paris, 1959, p. 319.

it totally. In so doing, his life achieves meaning and finds a stimulus in submission to the chosen idol. His enthusiasm does not arise, however, from the joy of the resulting relationship. It is an intense enthusiasm, but cold, built upon an interior death, or to put it symbolically, it is a 'burning ice.' "[5]

What is perhaps nothing but a pathological condition of the authentic religious dimension of man cannot then be made a *priori* absolute and objective.

In a brilliant conciliar intervention the Spanish Bishop, Monsignor Guerra, speaking of the possibility of a communist-catholic dialogue, made this acute observation: "Marxists should be invited to consider the tendency toward God not as an alienation, but as a dynamic perfection of man, precisely because they tend to recognize the fulness of human reality."

The marxists vis-a-vis the new facts

We notice, in fact, a tendency among some Marxist philosophers and writers to reconsider from first principles the whole problem of religious alienation. The avowedly marxist Italian novelist and movie-director Pier Paolo Passolini makes this remarkable statement: "There are two things that are certain: (1) an atheistic philosophy does not exclude respect for religion; (2) an atheistic philosophy is not the only possible philosophy for marxism."

In the Italian communist journal *Paese Sera* Francesco Valentini, in an article entitled *Communism and Religion*, also makes these affirmations: "Undoubtedly, the term anticlerical has become obsolete. Likewise the old militant atheism has abandoned the position of challenge to the truths of faith in the name of the truths of science as a lining up in direct opposition of the verifiable and the metaphysical. It will be said, naturally, that religious man belongs also to a church, e.g. the Catholic Church, which will impose on him not only beliefs and rites, but also moral and social duties. And this is obvious. But it is also obvious that the church as a sociological reality is one thing, and the church as community of salvation is another. And that the former is—as every member of the faithful knows—a worldly institution and therefore, subject to error. The believer is certainly not supposed to doubt

[5]E. Fromm, *Marx and his Conception of Man*, Fred Ungar Publishing Co., 1962, p. 55.

the Assumption of our Lady, but he may discuss for instance, the position of Msgr. Stepinac with regard to Ante Pavelic."

So deeply human is this search for transcendence, in which religiosity basically consists, that marxist philosophy itself has not been able to get rid of it, even though it has explicitly attempted to do so. The revisionist marxist philosopher Pierre Fougeyrollas accuses marxism of inconsistency in trying to give "meaning" to history. "The human intellect," writes Fougeyrollas, "does not seem to be capable of effecting such a discovery by itself. The affirmation of the meaning of history can be received as a revelation in the religious sense of the word. It cannot be the result of a scientific inquiry which is satisfied as soon as the ideal of a direction in history is proposed by way of hypothesis. Being a radical atheism, marxism forbids as such the recourse to religious revelation. Its pretension to discover a meaning in the historical event must be rejected and must provoke a serious examination of the metaphysical residues that it unwittingly carries with itself, and expose them for what they are."[6]

Must religion be the "opium of the people"?

In modern times many marxists are seriously asking themselves if the famous slogan must be understood in a strictly universal ("must religion be the opium of the people?") or in a temporary and episodical manner ("religion can be, and de facto has been, the opium of the people"). Those who deny the absolute universality of the slogan quote very definite texts of the classical marxists. Thus, for instance, Engels finds in his reading of the Apocalypse "a feeling that one is struggling against the whole world, and a certainty of victory."[7] And he writes on the epistles of St. John: "These letters exhort the faithful to be zealous in propaganda, to courageous and proud confession of their faith in face of the foe, to unrelenting struggle against the enemy both within and without—and as far as this goes they could just as well have been written by a prophetically minded enthusiast for the International."[8]

Engels himself does not limit this revolutionary aspect of the

[6]P. Fougeyrollas, *Le Marxisme en Question*, Paris, 1959, p. 91.

[7]K. Marx and F. Engels, *On Religion*, Schocken Books Inc., New York, 1964, p. 330.

[8]K. Marx and F. Engels, op. cit., p. 333.

evangelical message to primitive Christianity, but he sees it present all through Christianity's two thousand years.

The French marxist, Andre Moine, summarizes his study on this aspect of classical marxists: "We now want to sketch the broad conclusions that follow from the twofold permanent contradiction within the Church: her character of temporal power linked with the exploiters, and the presence of millions of exploited within herself. Throughout her history we find this double contradiction: there is a permanent struggle within the Church which is actually nothing but a reflection of the class struggle. At each historical stage there are ruptures between the rich and conservative hierarchy, guardian of the tradition the Church herself has forged, and some of the poor catholic masses in love with justice—at times revolutionary— who live in the memory of a just and vengeful Christ. If the class struggle is the motor of history that draws its power from the contradictions of society, in some circumstances and for some believers, religion is a justification and a stimulus to their struggles. It is the banner that guides the fight for social justice and freedom."[9]

Answering an objection in which Fr. Dubarle took for granted that atheism is the goal of marxism and of the governments based thereon, Moine himself answers bluntly: "Philosophical materialism cannot be identified with atheism. Our doctrine has nothing predetermined. It is the fruit of the accumulation of human knowledge and experience. In that source it constantly finds a new vigor, a new direction and new impulses around a solidly established and verified nucleus. Atheism is not our objective."[10]

The French marxist recognizes himself in the definition given by Teilhard de Chardin in 1945: "The first thing in marxism is not atheism, it is humanism, faith in man."

The Italian marxist, Lucio Lombardo Radice, speaks along the same lines. Starting with a thesis of the X Congress of the Italian Communist Party he positively affirms that "there can be a revolutionary impetus in religion, even in the present day."[11]

They have not arrived at this result, continues Lombardo Radice,

[9]A. Moine, *Apres Pacem in Terris, Communistes et Chrétiens*, Paris, Editions Sociales, 1965, pp. 78 ff.

[10]A. Moine, *op. cit.*, p. 152.

[11]L. Lombardo Radice, *Il Dialogo a la Prova*, Florence, Ed. Vallechi, 1964, p. 90.

through abstract reasoning but through the single and honest observation of historical facts. Religious men and women, motivated by religion, have contributed and continue to contribute effectively to the elimination of all human alienation, the religious one included. The Roman professor concludes with this sincere confession: "I honestly admit that I do not agree with Mario Gozzini that religion is a basic reality of the human spirit, and I am still convinced of Karl Marx's fourth thesis. But I am not at all interested in making *definitive* reasonings. Today religious forms are seen to be even capable of adopting progressive values. In that I am interested. That determines my theoretical judgment and my practical position. I refuse, therefore, to preach, as comrade Ilichov wanted, the war against God as being a condition for the necessary revolutionary transformation of society, and I believe, with Lenin, that "preaching war against God at all costs, as the anarchists criticized by Lenin used to do, would *de facto* help the priests (the reactionary clergy) and the bourgeosie."[12] Another Italian Marxist, Salvatore di Marco, also makes the following sincere and daring confession:

> "I must confess that the theory of religious alienation, in the form in which it can be deduced from the classical philosophy of Marxism, creates many problems for me, because it has been shown to apply only to certain historical conditions. Is it always true that the need for religion is born in man as an unconscious projection into the transcendent of 'impossible' earthly needs? Is that all we Marxists understand when we say that the idea of God is a human representation? The experience of a certain type of advance Italian Catholicism tells us that such is not always the case. The believer often finds in his faith ideal reasons for a profound historic commitment. These reasons enable him to express progressive content in a religious form."[13]

Likewise, the Spanish marxist, Manuel Azcarate, makes a similar exegesis of the marxist slogan: "Having established this, another question comes up before the marxist: is religion just an 'opium'? We do not think so. It is necessary to probe a little deeper than we have done so far into this idea (expressed by Marx in the text given above) which represents religion as a *protest* against the abandonment of man. This conception is reflected in other classical works of Marxism. It is a fundamental aspect without which a

[12]L. Lombardo Radice, *op. cit.*, p. 122.
[13]*Ibid.*, p. 422.

series of historical (and modern also!) events would escape our understanding."[14]

We do not wish to discuss some minor points of the value judgments we have just quoted. We are only interested in pointing out the clear and convincing fact that truly representative marxist humanists categorically affirm that: (a) religion is not necessarily the opium of the people; (b) religion can be, and de facto has been and still is, an impulse and stimulus to human development; (c) a "militant atheism," understood as an a priori and merciless struggle against any form of religion, is not at all demanded by the dynamism of the socialist praxis.

Biological significance of pauline morality

Consistent with its principles, marxist morality has attempted to refuse any search for transcendental and extrinsic values which, from above and outside, would become a pole of attraction and a road to be followed in moral action. Its materialism consists in denying the transcendency of values as interests and necessities. Marxist ethics, however, just like artistic creation, has not been able to prescind, de facto, from the perspective of an ideal. Recently some post-marxist philosophers, that is to say, those who started out as marxists and who continue to be richly nourished by its doctrine, have submitted to harsh criticism this aseptic quality claimed by marxist ethics. "Marxism," writes Fougeyrollas, "has not been able to get rid of all value judgments, and the revolutionary movements it inspired have been based psychologically on data that have nothing to do with simple needs or simple interests. The revolutionary militant who agrees to lead a heroic life is moved by a force that cannot be reduced to the interests or needs of the working class or the consciousness of historical necessity. In consequence, the workers' movement is itself a witness to the intrinsic difficulties of the marxist doctrine of values. The existence of revolutionary militants who have sacrificed their personal and family interests for their ideal, shows that some ethical values without transcendental foundation have been passionately cultivated, but they are not reducible to economic or social interests or needs."[15]

This pendular swing between the blind acceptance of some

[14]Manuel Azcarate, quoted in *Realidad*, May 5, 1965, p. 18.
[15]P. Fougeyrollas, *op. cit.*, p. 113 ff.

transcendental values which absorb and nullify man's ethical effort, and the desperate effort to escape from those values in order to face oneself, does not attain stability at either extreme. The recent disappointment of the post-Marxist philosophers shows this quite well.

Simone de Beauvoir describes this ambiguous situation, one that is characteristic of man's moral effort. "Ever since there were men and they began to live," she writes, "all have experienced this tragic ambiguity in their condition. But ever since philosophers first began to think, the majority have attempted to disguise it. They have struggled to reduce the spirit to matter or to reabsorb matter in the spirit, or to fuse both in a unique substance. Those who have accepted dualism have established a hierarchy between body and soul that enabled them to consider as worthless the part of themselves that could not be saved. They have denied death, either integrating it into life or considering it as a veil of illusion under which the truth of a Nirvana is hidden. And the moral they propose to their disciples always aims at the same goal: they attempt to suppress the ambiguity either by becoming pure interiority or pure exteriority, escaping from the world of the senses or submerging themselves in it, approaching eternity or locking themselves in the confines of the present instant."[16]

Simone de Beauvoir's observation is acute. It describes the whole core of the axiological motivation of ethics throughout the history of ideas. Ever since Plato, suppression of this radical ambiguity of human nature has been attempted in our western world in order to find transcendental values capable of polarizing man's ethical activity. According to Plato, the soul has been united to the body through some sort of violence against its nature. The body is for the soul a prison from which it must be liberated.[17] For this reason, the wise man—the only virtuous man—far from fearing death greets it with hope, because he expects from it the fulfillment of the work to which he has dedicated his whole life.[18]

Aristotle, following the same line, reduces the whole grandeur of moral life to a lonely and introvert position of contemplation. Happiness—the only objective of the ethical effort—consists in the contemplative life.[19]

---

[16]S. de Beauvoir, *Pour une Morale de l'Ambiguité*, Ed. Gallimard, 1962, p. 10.
[17]Plato, *Phedon*, 65A–67B; 82D–83E; *Republic*, 611B–612A; *Phaedrus*, 250C.
[18]*Phedo*, 66B–69B; cfr. 80D–84B; 114D–115A.
[19]Aristotle, *Ethics*, X, 7, 1.177 (a.12–21).

The highest degree of this contemplation can be attained only after death, when the soul finds itself and sees itself completely free from any corporeal ties. For this reason the aristotelian ethics undertakes a road of evasion and escape from any temporal and material commitment.

A morality of reconciliation with the body, the world, and material things seems to begin with the Stoics. The Stoic slogan "to live according to nature"[20] not only refers to human reason itself, but to the totality of things. Life in itself, however, is not considered either good or evil. Thus we have the right to abandon it when it no longer offers the conditions that will allow virtue to develop favorably.[21] As usual the ambiguity of the human condition is destroyed with an evident detriment to the body and to the world context of human existence.

Finally Plotinus makes use of this whole hellenistic tradition to construct his system of morality, or better yet, his mystique of total purification. The soul acquires wings when it is separated from the matter which oppresses it and hinders the deployment of all its power.[22] As opposed to the Stoics, Plotinus does not hold for suicide. Each one must wait for his assigned time, when the body is naturally separated from the soul as the ripe fruit falls from the tree.[23] The separation of soul from body must be an internal separation, a purification. Moral life consists in purification. According to ancient wisdom, Plotinus concludes, all virtue is nothing but a purification, through which the soul is liberated from the body and becomes like to God.[24]

This morality of purification, resolving the ambiguity of the human condition in favor of the spirit and against matter, has appeared frequently present in our western civilization. It has succeeded in penetrating deeply into Christian ethics and Christian mysticism, as well. The criticism that marxism has recently made of this spiritual inflation of morality, which places ethics simply and totally at the service of the religious ideologies, especially that

---

[20]*Homologoumenos te physei zen*, Diogenes, LVII, 87; Cicero, *De Finibus*, IV, 6,4: "*Convenienter naturae vivere.*"

[21]It is the *eulogos exagoge*, Diogenes, LVII, 130; cfr. Cicero, *De Finibus*, III, 18, 60–61; Seneca, *Epistles*, 12, 10; Marcus Aurelius, X, 8.

[22]Plotinus, I, 8 and 14.

[23]Plotinus, I, 9.

[24]Plotinus, I, 2; cfr. book VII, chapter 6.

of Christianity, forces us to revise patiently and honestly the axiology
of biblical morality.

With this intention I have gathered in chronological order some
Pauline texts in which the acceptance of the total ambiguity of
the human condition emerges as an indisputable fact—an ambiguity
which man's moral effort, illumined and empowered by grace, will
only overcome in an authentic dialectic of opposites: body and
soul, matter and spirit, in a final, inclusive synthesis, whose context
will be worldly and divine at the same time.

Pauline texts

1 Thes. 1.9–10: "It is recorded of us what a welcome we had
among you, and how you turned to God from idols, to serve a
living a true God, and to await his Son from heaven, whom he
raised from the dead, Jesus who delivers us from the wrath to come."

Chronologically this is the first text in which Paul presents—
only in kernel form—an obsessive idea that will permeate his whole
"morality." It has to do with a "conversion," a moral position—
"to serve God"—and it is based on the "expectation of the *parousia*."
In this epistle Paul develops his thought on the *Parousia,* linking
it intrinsically with the eschatological resurrection of the believers.
(4:13–18) Besides, the "resurrection of Jesus *from among the
dead*" is mentioned explicitly as the supreme motivation for the
"service of God."

1 Thes. 5.8–11: "But since we belong to the day, let us be sober,
and put on the breastplate of faith and love, and for a helmet the
hope of salvation. For God has not destined us for wrath, but to
gain salvation through our Lord Jesus Christ, who died for us
in order that whether we wake or sleep we may find life in union
with him. Therefore, encourage one another and build one another
up, as you are doing."

Now we face a moral exhortation. Night is ordinarily the time
of many inadmissible actions. Day, because of its brightness, does
not lend itself to immoral behavior. In order to exhort effectively
to morally worthy behavior Paul refers to the "hope of salvation."
This salvation, however, refers explicitly to the eschatological resurrection. Indeed the expression to be "awake" or to "sleep" is not
used here in the literal sense (v.7) or in the metaphorical sense
of v.6. With these two verbs Paul designates the two conditions

in which believers will find themselves at the coming of the Lord: some will be alive, some will be dead. (4.13–18) But the difference between these two situations is not important, because the purpose of the redemptive death of Christ is that his own, dead or alive, through his resurrection or transfiguration "may find life in union with him."

1 Cor 3:10–15: "According to the commission God has given me, like a skilled master builder I laid a foundation, and another man is building upon it. Let each man take care how he builds upon it. For no other foundation can any one lay than the one already laid, which is Jesus Christ. Now if any one builds on the foundation with gold, silver, precious stones, wood, hay, stubble, each man's world will be made manifest; for the Day will disclose it, because fire will reveal it, and the fire will test what sort of work each one has done. If the work which any man has built on the foundation survives, he will receive a reward. If any man's work is burned up, he will suffer a loss, yet he himself will be saved, but only as through fire."

This is an exhortation to overcome the danger of sectarianism (3–4) To do so, Paul teaches positively how Christians must carry out this task of constructing the Church. This task presupposes an "effort," "work" (*kopos*, v.8). This effort must produce an *objective* success whose end will coincide with the "consummation." The salvation of the individual will not necessarily coincide with the task objectively accomplished. The man who is of good faith, but mistaken in his technique of construction, will not be excluded from the Kingdom of God, but the Kingdom of God would not have really been built had there not been builders endowed with an objectively efficient technique.

This pauline idea is the basis of the "vital" motivation of some moral exhortations in his correspondence with the Corinthians.

1 Cor 6:13–14: "Food is for the stomach and the stomach is for food—and God will destroy both one and the other. The body is not for immorality, but for the Lord, and the Lord for the body. Just as God raised the Lord, so he will raise us by his power."

Paul, using the hellenistic "debate" device, assumes an objection from his interlocutor: "Corporeal life is ephemeral. The dialectic food-stomach is transient, and God himself will bring it to an end." This is a typically Greek conception. The only interesting thing is the spirit that remains. The body is something provisional and not important. Therefore, lust and other carnal excesses cannot soil the spirit, the only heir of the Kingdom of God. Paul counters by placing in the center of moral motivation faith in corporeal resurrection. The body is defined by a religious relationship with the Lord (in Paul *Kyrios* emphasizes the idea of the risen Christ). The risen Christ—the redeemer—has an active relationship with the human body, which is not something transient or disposable. Quite the contrary! The body will be raised up as a consequence of the resurrection of Christ. In Christianity there is a sexual morality precisely because of the eschatological importance granted to the body. This fundamental consideration will straighten out many deviations from sane sexual morality based virtually on the Greek pejorative concept of the body.

1 Cor 15:16–19; 30–32, 58: "If the dead are not raised, Christ has not been raised. But if Christ has not been raised, your faith is groundless and you are still in your sins! Then those also who have fallen asleep in Christ, are lost. If for this life only we have hoped in Christ, we are of all men most to be pitied.

"If the dead are not raised, why am I in peril every hour? I protest brethren, by my pride in you which I have in Christ Jesus our Lord, that day after day I face death! What do I gain if, humanly speaking, I fought with beasts at Ephesus? If the dead are not raised, 'Let us eat and drink, since tomorrow we die.'

"Therefore, my beloved brothers, be steadfast, immovable, always abounding in the work of the Lord, realizing that in the Lord your labor is not in vain."

Faith, for Paul, as in the rest of the Bible as well, is a vital attitude that commits the whole man and consists essentially in accepting the divine gift of salvation in order to attain man's fulfillment. This is why the content of the human-divine dialogue of faith is the resurrection of Christ as the first fruit and guarantee of the resurrection of the believers. Therefore if Christ has not risen, there will be no general resurrection and our faith will have no content: we would be leaning on a vacuum, or leaping into a bottomless abyss. The situation prior to faith is one of sin, since sin is an objective climate. "Everything that does not proceed from faith is sin" (Rom 14:23).

Without resurrection those "who died in Christ" will come to "perdition" in eternal death. Clearly the state immediately following death is considered as a situation of non-salvation. The inference is clear. Since the existence of the separated soul is not "life," we would have—in case there is no resurrection—to limit our Christian hope to this life. Such a "hope" seems to Paul pitiful and inadmissible.

Likewise the apostolic "spirituality" is governed by the hope of a corporeal resurrection. Paul defines the professional apostle as "one that lives in constant peril." He himself has had a hard struggle in his task of evangelizing Ephesus, even to having been at the brink of death. The professional apostle faces this danger only because he has confidence in the resurrection. Were it not so, it would not be worth risking his life. Instead, he should make the best of it, following the Epicurean aphorism: "Eat and drink, for tomorrow we shall die."

The whole of Chapter 15 is devoted to the resurrection. It ends with an exhortation to take a firm stand on the side of moral behavior and to take this stand with a confident hope of achieving an objective success, which is neither more nor less than the resurrection of the body.

2 Cor 1:8–10: "We do not want you to be ignorant, brethren, of the affliction which befell us in Asia; for we were so utterly, unbearably crushed that we despaired of life itself. Why, we had within ourselves the sentence of death; but that was to make us rely not on ourselves but on God who raises the dead. He it is who delivered us from such deadly peril, and is now delivering us; on him we have set our hope that he will deliver us again."

Paul, despite his submission to God's will, does not want to die. He wants to stretch his existence to a maximum. However, he will accept death in hope of the resurrection. And if now he is being freed of some mortal dangers, resulting from the apostolic adventure, he attributes it to the God who will raise him up from the dead, who is partially anticipating the great eschatological rehabilitation of life.

2 Cor 4:14, 16–18: "We are convinced that he who raised Jesus will raise us also with Jesus and place us near him with you. . . . So we do not lose heart. Though our outer nature is wasting away, our inner nature is being renewed every day. For our present light affliction is producing for us an eternal weight of glory that is

beyond all measure, while we look not to the things that are seen but to the things that are unseen. What we see is temporary, but what we do not see endures forever."

"Overlooking the context, verses 16–18 could have well been written by Philo (or any other Platonist). He also distinguishes the invisible world (considered perfect and lasting) from the visible one. And the opposition between the two men—exterior and interior—even reminds us of the Hermetic terminology. However, considering the totality of the Apostle's doctrine, we have to read this passage from the eschatological point of view, something unacceptable to Platonists and Hermetics."[25]

Paul distinguishes a constant and progressive tension between the "external" and the "internal human condition." This dialectic has to be understood in the framework of pauline anthropology, which never divides man into "body" and "soul" but into "flesh" and "spirit." Flesh is the situation of man when left to his own resources with a certain emphasis on God's absence. Here the "external human condition" coincides more or less with the "flesh." The "ruin of the flesh" is in direct proportion with the "salvation of the spirit" (1 Cor 5:5). Since man is a "dual" being, he is simultaneously subject to the action of "flesh" or "death," and to the action of "spirit" or "life." "So you also must consider yourselves dead to sin and alive to God in Christ Jesus" (Rom 6:11).

Therefore the concrete action of the "spirit" on the Christian, even though it may seem paradoxically destructive, has as counterpart a progressive influence toward a "glorious" end. Naturally, this glorious end is nothing but the corporeal resurrection explicitly affirmed in v.14.

Affliction (*thlipsis*) is in Paul a constructive element. The Church is built with affliction. This is not a Buddhist or Hellenic concept. It is a fact that the resistance of evil can be overcome only through a bloody battle. This alone is what justifies the presence of affliction in Christian existence. We need it for the progressive construction of the Church in the midst of the human family.

Therefore affliction in its apparently degrading action upon man has a deeply influential counterbalance in the deepest part of man's being: the eschatological resurrection.

25J. Héring, *La Seconde Épître de Saint Paul aux Corinthiens*, Neuchâtel-Paris, 1958, p. 45.

These reflections support the paradoxical lesson of the stormy life of the apostles (4:8–10).

Phil 3:10–21: "I would know Christ and the power of his resurrection. I would also share in his sufferings, in the hope that, if I resembled him in death, I may somehow attain to the resurrection from the dead. Not that I have already obtained this ideal, or have already been made perfect, but I press on hoping to make it my own, because Christ Jeus has made me his own. Brethren, I do not consider that I have made it my own; but one thing I do; forgetting what is past, I strain toward what is ahead. . . . I press on to the prize in store for those who have received from above God's call in Jesus Christ. Let those of us who are mature be thus minded; and if in any point you disagree, in this God will enlighten you. Only let us hold true to what we have attained.

"Brethren, join in imitating me, and mark those who so live as you have an example in us. For many, of whom I have often told you and now tell you even with tears, live as enemies of the cross of Christ. Their end is ruin, their god is their belly, their glory is in their shame, with minds set on earthly things. As for us, our commonwealth is in heaven, and from there it is that we await a Savior, the Lord Jesus Christ, who will change our lowly body to be like his glorious body, by the power which enables him even to subject all things to himself."

Here Paul deals with moral behavior (*peripatountas symmimetai*) which he compares with a race. The finish line of this "race" is precisely the resurrection of the body. The "communion with the suffering of Christ" brings man, it is true, to death, though not to a purely biological death, but rather "a death like Christ's." The only motive for our joining in the suffering and death of Christ is simply the participation in reverse in this "moral" aspect: the resurrection. "Without any other aim but that of arriving at the resurrection." The judaizers preach an introvert morality, all of it reduced to determining what meals are pure or impure, according to a complicated legal code. For them God is in the long run the stomach. "Shame" (*aischine*) refers to the sexual organ.[26] Paul uses an incisive irony: they base their glory on a part of the body considered

[26]Cfr. 1 Kgs 20:30 LXX; Nah. 3:5; Is 20:4; Ez 16:36–37; 22; 29. In the New Testament, Apoc 3:18.

shameful. Here there is a play on the words: the opposite of "glorifying himself" (*doksazesthai*) is to "be confounded" (*aischinesthai*).

Gal 6:7–9: "Be not deceived. God is not mocked. A man reaps just what he sows. Yes, he who sows in his corrupt nature, from that corrupt nature reaps corruption; but he who sows in the field of the Spirit will from the Spirit reap eternal life. And let us not grow weary in well-doing, for in due season we shall reap, if we do not lose heart."

The moral behavior of the Christian moves toward an eschatological end. A man who has preferred to live in the proud solitude of his flesh, will not be able to reap any other harvest but "corruption." We are in an eschatological context—"divine judgment"— parallel to that of 1 Cor 15:35–38. There he also speaks of "sowing" (36–37), of "corruption" (*phthora*, 42, 51, 53; *phtharton*, 53). The "corruption" refers clearly to the "corporeal death" and the "incorruption" to the eschatological resurrection (v.53).

Paul means that man's sinful behavior—the *kauchesis*, the remaining-in-the-flesh—not only separates him from God morally, but puts him on the track toward an eschatological result of complete existential failure: the "corruption," the "eternal death," the total loss of hope in "living." On the contrary, the morally good behavior of the Christian not only makes him pleasing to God, but biologically puts him on the road for his full existential maturity: "eternal life," the eschatological resurrection.

The parallel with 1 Cor is even closer in the last phrase (v.9). As in that passage, Paul insists here that the final result—the resurrection—is the only thing that makes the lofty Christian morality reasonable. That is why he again stresses the theme of effectiveness with expressions similar to those of 1 Cor 15:58. The human effort not only has the extrinsic value of merit, through which it deserves a reward. Provided it has been elevated through its union with Christ (*en Kyrio*), it also achieves results of human fullness which achieve a complete justification of the whole worldly performance of historical man.

Rom 5:1–5: "Since we are justified by faith, we have peace with God through our Lord Jesus Christ. Through him we have found entrance into this state of grace in which we now abide, and expect in the hope of participating in God's glory. More than that, we rejoice in our sufferings, knowing that suffering produces endurance, and endurance produces character, and character produces hope, and hope does not disappoint us, because God's love has been poured forth in our hearts by the Holy Spirit who has been given to us."

Christian morality follows this route: tribulation—perseverance—authenticity—hope. This hope, it is clear, is "of the glory of God." The "glory" in an eschatological reality and is intrinsically bound up with resurrection. (1 Cor 2:7; 15:43; 2 Cor 4:17; Phil 3:21; Rom 8:17; Rom 8:18–21; Col. 3:4; 2 Tim 2:10).

Rom 6:19c–23: "Just as you once offered your members to impurity and to greater and greater iniquity, so now you offer your members to righteousness for sanctification. When you were the slaves of sin, you rendered no service to holiness. But what advantage had you then from those things of which you are now ashamed? The end of those things is death. But now, set free from sin and become slaves of God, have your reward in sanctification, and its end, eternal life. For the wages of sin is death, but the free gift of God is life everlasting in Christ Jesus our Lord."

The value judgment that in the long run makes the road of immorality impossible refers to the "resurrectional" incapacity of that way of acting. The slave of sin is greatly disappointed in the end. His "ruler" rewards only with "death" whereas the person who practices Christian morality knows that he in the end will be rewarded with "eternal life." This eternal life is clearly the resurrection which in this sense is the theme of the whole chapter.

Rom 8:5–6, 12–13, 17–18: "Those who live according to the flesh set their minds on the things of the flesh, but those who live according to the Spirit set their minds on the things of the Spirit. To set the mind on the flesh is death, but to set the mind on the Spirit is life and peace.

"So then, brethren, we are debtors, not to the flesh, to live according to the flesh—for if you live according to the flesh you will die, but if by the Spirit you put to death the deeds of the body you will live.

"If we are children, then heirs, heirs of God and fellow heirs with Christ, provided we suffer with him in order that we may also be glorified with him. I consider that the sufferings of this present time are not worthy to be compared with the glory that is to be revealed to us."

The theme of this passage is moral behavior (to walk, *peripatein*). The "deeds of the body": "body" is the whole man in his external and visible performance. Here it refers to man-in-himself, insofar as he tries to act on his own. The Christian discards this manner of action (*praxis*) and "puts it to death aware that this road leads straight to death."

The "glory" to which this moral behavior will lead is clearly the corporeal resurrection, placed at the end of history and enveloped in the consummation or completion of creation itself (19:20). In Genesis, 1:1, man is shown as the meaning given by God to his total creative work. He is made responsible for creation, which he is entrusted with bringing to a successful completion, through a work carried out in dependence on God. It seems that "the one that subjected it" is God himself (v.20), who in a positive manner, through making man responsible for creation, has subjected the created universe to the risk involved in man's freedom. This submission to human destiny decreed by God is, however, subject to one condition: hope in a future liberation. The metaphor taken from the pains of childbirth (v.22) indicates that the "transcendental destiny" given by God to creation is not discontinuous or prefabricated. It is intimately related to the evolving reality of a world carrying in its womb another world. The new world will not be totally different, although it will supersede the former one in its fullness.

In conclusion, from the reading of these texts, it follows: (a) that Christian ethics is intrinsically governed by an essential connection with the future eschatological resurrection; (b) that between the present action and the final consummation there is an evolving history and a continuous transition; (c) that man's active participation is an intrinsic element in the history or evolution of creation; (d) that therefore the Christian's behavior must extend to the whole evolutionary reality of history. All of it must be imbued with "grace" to find the right road to "salvation."

In brief, the "salvation" to which "grace" or the gift of God refers, includes essentially and intrinsically the final and definitive rehabilitation of the "life" of man's body together with its inseparable cosmic context.

A pastoral doctrine of non-alienation

In concluding these theological reflections we will now examine a problem of pastoral practice which must never be neglected in any worthwhile study of the biblical message. As we have seen, the biblical God is a gratuitous God who must never be confused with the intrinsic structure of the human adventure. We Christians—the Church—are the messengers of a gratuitous God. It is necessary, therefore, to present this message of gratuity in a climate of absolute gratuity. The Church must always flee from the grave danger of presenting herself to men as an essential and intrinsic component of social behavior. The religious option must always be really free. It must never be contaminated with other temporal commitments. This is just what Vatican Council II affirmed in its Constitution on the Church in the Modern World: "The Church disapproves of discrimination between believers and unbelievers, and of the fact that some governments, not recognizing the fundamental rights of human person, contradict them unjustly." Not having presented a gratuitous God, we believers have become responsible for atheism (according to the expression of the Constitution) because "we have hidden the true face of God and religion rather than revealed it."

"Give without pay, what you received without pay" (Mt 10:8). This was Christ's first pastoral exhortation when he "sent" his disciples to preach the good news. But very often the air of sufficiency and pride in our preaching has emptied the kerygma of its salvific gratuity. A preacher of the transcendent gratuity must appear to men in an attitude of humility, and even with an inferiority complex. Antonio Machado has described this attitude toward truth very well in a marvelous stanza:

> "Your truth? No! The truth.
> Come with me to searching for it.
> You keep yours."

This is the same rule that controlled the first presentation of the Kerygma to our western world. Paul wrote to the Corinthians: "But we preach Christ crucified, a stumbling block for the Jews, and folly to Gentiles. But to those that are called—both Jews and Greeks—Christ, the power of God, and the wisdom of God" (1 Cor 1:23–24).

The "Jews" of today are precisely the conservative Christians deeply rooted in their "religious answers," perfectly clear, cut and dried, in short, "immanentized." For them it is a stumbling block to see evaporate in their very hands the beautiful "deist" apologetics, with which they had patiently tamed God and with which they had prepared a place for him (certainly the place of honor) at the round table of their decisions.

The modern "Greeks" could be all those who believe that the death of God is intimately connected with man's progressive development. To these "Greeks," we twentieth century Christians continue to declare honestly that we have absolutely no desire to present ourselves as rivals to the autonomy—both intellectual and practical— of Prometheus. Our message remains the same: a "folly," something totally gratuitous, not demanded at all by historical and concrete human reality.

After the confession of our "Christian paradox" we humbly ask our atheistic brethren to try to understand our radical allergy to any kind of alienation, especially religious alienation.

We also ask them to let us believe and announce humbly and helpfully that "for us—Jews and Greeks—who have been called, Christ is the power of God and wisdom of God." And above all we ask them not to feel hurt if we Christians, as Peter said, "are always ready to make defense to any that calls us to account for the hope that there is in us" (1 Pe 3:15).

This means that a Christian who, finding support in his own principles, sincerely affirms that he is ready to struggle against any form of religious alienation, cannot be kept from joining in the common effort for the upward thrust of the human *praxis*.

On the other hand, if, as a condition for joining, the unbelievers insist on rejection of the Christian faith or demand a conviction— not empirical but metaphysical—that the same *praxis* in its evolution will eliminate inescapably the residues of faith, we can regard this position as an authentic alienation. The reason is that such a condition would keep a great number of believers from the construction of the world that has to be. These masses have an obligation and a right (even in virtue of their own faith) to participate in the constructive *praxis* of the new imminent reality.

The heart of the matter is that the dialogue between these human- ists and Christians is still confined to the one subject of the sincerity of both groups, while we are faced with the reality of the urgent need to build a world from which can be banished the present human alienations.

But in a second stage, when participation in the common task is effected the dialogue will be neeeded not between humanists and Christians, but between believers and unbelievers. Such a dialogue will not interfere at all with the progress of human *praxis*. The loyal and sincere collaboration will ensure its safety.

Only when the atmosphere has been thus clarified will we be able to talk of a God totally gratuitous and at the same time saving.

PART III

THE CHURCH,

PEOPLE OF GOD

IN THE

WORLD

CHAPTER 8

MISSIONARY URGENCY AND SENSE OF HISTORY IN THE THEOLOGY OF PAUL

In a talk to the *Paulus-Gesellschaft* (Society of St. Paul) in Frankfurt, the renowned German theologian, Karl Rahner, stresses that the modern concept of "salvation of the unbelievers" goes beyond the existential framework in which Paul worked when he hastened to bring the message of salvation to all the corners of the known world.

"As Christians of this century in the Church, we can no longer think so pessimistically of the salvation of non-Christians as Paul could within the religious outlook of his age and as Christians could still do as late as the seventeenth century. For Paul, those who did not receive baptism were lost. True, he did not propound any dogma about this. But in practice this was, for him, something obvious. This was the perspective within which he did his missionary work. Right on to the late Middle Ages and beyond, Christians to a large extent derived their missionary impulse from this view. We as Christians of the twentieth century can no longer conform to this perspective and practice. Indeed, we must not. A missionary today can no longer hold the conviction that, say, Francis Xavier still had: 'If I go to the Japanese and teach them and preach Christ to them, they will be saved and go to heaven; but if I stay in Europe, they will be lost, as their forefathers were lost, because they never heard of Christ and died without baptism.' Thus something has penetrated into our religious sense, something that does not in the least need to involve lukewarmness or anything un-Christian. But we have got to acknowledge that our missionary impulse has suffered by it; that it no longer has the intensity that it had in earlier ages of the Church's history."[1]

The solution proposed by Rahner to this difficulty or objection to the missionary impulse can be stated simply as follows: "Now I know, from the teachings of my faith that God gives every man as much grace as he needs to save himself. God wills that all men should be saved, says St. Paul. But it may be God's will that I should intervene in favour of this particular man. If I fail, no doubt God will give him grace even without me. God writes straight with crooked lines. The ultimate depth of grace is revealed in this, that God lets good come out of evil. But woe to the man who thinks that this means he can usurp God's position: that he can do evil that good may come. Woe to that man who thinks that he can outwit God. But this is what we should be trying to do if we made the possibility of salvation outside God's normal means of salvation into a basis for the conclusion that we have no apostolic task, or no urgent one: that God has no need of us human beings."[2]

From this assumed soteriologic point of view we could deduce that the salvation of humanity can be totally independent of the action of the Church, the latter thus being reduced to a function of a society for the facilitation of salvation. Is this Paul's concept?

The road to individual salvation is open to any man of good will

In the first place, to say that Paul taught that those who have not heard the gospel are not on the road to salvation is totally unacceptable.

We will limit ourselves to some fundamental pauline texts concerning this point taken from the first three chapters of the letter to the Romans. Paul begins by describing the religious world which today we would call "natural" and which for him was the Greco-Roman world.

The dialectic God-man is normally found in this world. God is manifested as an "eternal power" and as a "divine Lordship" through contingent reality. This manifestation of God can be followed by man's acceptance, and by his subsequent moral behavior in the light of his own reflection. Therefore the accusing judgment of God

[1] K. Rahner, *Mission and Grace*, Sheed and Ward, London, 1966, Vol. III, p. 6–7.
[2] K. Rahner, *op. cit.*, p. 14.

falls, in this "naturally" religious world, only on those who consciously and culpably have kept that known truth from becoming a derived moral *praxis*. Here are the pauline texts.

"The wrath of God is being revealed from heaven against all ungodliness and wickedness of those men who in wickedness stifle the truth of God. For what can be known about God is plain to them, because God has manifested it to them. Ever since the creation of the world his invisible nature, namely, his eternal power and deity, has been clearly perceived in the things that have been made. So they are without excuse; for although they knew God they did not honor him as God or give thanks, but they became futile in their thinking and their senseless minds were darkened" (Rom 1:18–21).

Paul addresses primarily the intellectuals responsible for the situation. "And since they did not see fit to acknowledge God, God gave them to a base mind and to improper conduct" (Rom 1:28). Moreover, they were guilty not only because they did immoral deeds against their conscience, but because they "approved those who practiced such things" (Rom 1:32). That is, they did not fulfill their prophetic mission as responsible intellectual leaders to preach boldly the truth they possessed.

Proceeding a little farther into this universal rule of salvation, Paul announces the general principle. Before the tribunal of the definitive judgment of God every individual will be judged according to the degree of purity of his own conscience. "By your hard and impenitent heart you are storing up wrath for yourself on the day of wrath when God's righteous judgment will be revealed. For he will render to every man according to his works: to those who by impatience in well-doing seek for glory and honor and immortality, he will give eternal life; but for those who are factious and who do not submit to the truth, but assent to iniquity, there will be wrath and fury. Tribulation and anguish shall be the lot of every man who is bent on evil-doing, the Jew first and then of the Greek; but glory, and honor, and peace will be the lot of every man intent on doing good, the Jew first and then of the Greek, since with God there is no favoritism" (Rom 2:5–11).

And for this general law to be fulfilled, in which the "Greeks" had been specifically included, he explicitly repeats his view that outside this area of positive revelation there is a normal development of the process of individual salvation: "Whoever have sinned, not having the Law, will perish without respect to the Law, and whoever were bound by the Law and have sinned, will be judged by the Law. For it is not the hearers of the Law who are righteous before God, but the doers of the Law who will be justified. When the Gentiles who have no law follow the dictates of reason and do what the Law prescribes, these, though they have no law are a law to themselves. They show that the requirements of the law are written in their hearts. Their conscience bears the same testimony, as also their thoughts which alternately accuse or defend them. This will be evident on the day when, according to my gospel, God will judge the secrets of men by Christ Jesus" (Rom 2:12–16).

The apostle judges this position of the natural man before God to be so valid that even his own relations with him are understood in terms of faith: "For in the manifestation of the proclamation of the Good News, the favorable judgment of God is revealed from faith to faith, as it is written, 'he who through faith is righteous shall live'" (Rom 1:17). The gospel is in fact the proclamation of the good news with regard to the certainty of man's salvation. And this event of the proclamation of the good news of God's righteousness is "revealed" (*apokalyptetai*), that is, reaches its greatest clarity. The Greek verb corresponds to the Hebrew *gaeáh* and does not refer to "an intellectual type of knowledge, but to an intuitive contact with the message hidden in transcendence, especially when the term is used to mean the immanentization of pre-existing transcendental realities."[3] This *apokalypsis* is more than a "revelation," an "apparition," or a breaking-in of the transcendent into the immanent. Paul means by this that even from the beginning God had conceived a plan for man's salvation, but its fulfillment was achieved only with the proclamation of the Good News. With the gospel, the first step in salvation and its first fruit have been inaugurated in the first Man saved: Jesus Christ, both saved and savior. The resurrection of Christ is the climax of all the favorable judgments God had been passing on mankind in the development of his evolving plan.

If the gospel is thus the midday glory of this favorable judgment, it is clear that even before it, God was already manifesting himself to

---

[3]A. Oepke, *Theologisches Wörterbuch zum Neuen Testament*, III, p. 579

man and offering him salvation. God's manifestation to the pagans takes place, according to Paul, when they recognize their own weakness and accept a God who gratuitiously offers the remedy for that weakness. Hence if in the God-man dialectic there is a progession on the part of God's favorable judgment, which from an incipient and initial stage achieves fulness in the guaranteeing fact of Christ's resurrection, why not assume that on the part of man's acceptance there is also an ascending scale?

Paul seems to be referring to this when he asserts that the "righteous judgment of God" reaches, in the gospel, its maximum fullness from faith to faith. When man accepts this salvific judgment of God, based on the resurrection of Christ, his faith—his acceptance —has also achieved some sort of fullness. The inference is that the acceptance of a man outside the gospel was also a type of faith, although incipient and elementary.

Indeed, faith in the whole Old Testament refers primarily not to the strictly revealed content of the divine message, but to the simple acceptance of God as savior of the human weakness, even though this "manifestation of God" is made only through the normal channels of purely human reflection.

If we had to reduce this idea to scholastic precision we could say that the faith of the man outside the gospel is not supernatural so far as the content of the message is concerned, but only with regard to the intrinsic grace that supports it and makes it possible. In brief, the purely natural human world does not exist, and *de facto* has never existed. All is grace and all is faith. Having made this clear Paul goes on to resolve the doubt that immediately assails us: if everything outside the Gospel is grace and faith, why the Gospel at all?

Salvation: "divine mystery" or sacrament of history

On this issue Paul follows the clear directive of the Old Testament. Israel's mission was not directly linked with the individual salvation which always comes up in our consideration of the subject. In the most relevant "missionary" texts it is understood that the Gentiles know God without need for preaching on the part of Israel, and the prophets themselves direct their charges against the Gentiles, blaming them for their defection from God. What they never do is to urge them to be converted to Israel.

"Actually," writes R. Martin-Archard, "Israel has no other mission vis-à-vis the pagans, than to be the chosen people. Only as a holy nation, consecrated to God, will Israel reflect his glory and bear witness to his holiness. In this way, by its presence in the world, it takes on a mediating function. Through it Yawheh will manifest his sovereignty and will make his word heard. The task entrusted to the chosen people thus assumes three complementary aspects. It has to communicate the divine oracle, to speak in the name of Yawheh and to bear witness to his kingship over creation. In brief, the eschatological mission of Israel with respect to the world consists in assuming the roles of priest, prophet and king. What Moses was for Israel itself in a decisive moment of its history, the people of Yahweh will be for mankind when God institutes his messianic era."[4]

This is exactly Paul's vision. After having recognized that circumcision is not necessary for "individual salvation" (Rom 2:25-29) he turns to the problem of the reason for Israel's existence as a chosen people. "Then what advantage has a Jew, or what is the value of circumcision? Much, in every respect. To begin with, the Jews are entrusted with the oracles of God" (Rom 3:1-2). In short, the superiority of Israel does not refer to the concrete reality of being in a favorable situation with respect to the problem of individual salvation, but to a historical mission on which will depend the final outcome of that history of salvation. In order to understand properly the pauline thought on this subject we have to grasp it in a theme to which he returns frequently, namely, the progressive history of creation as mystery of God.

Following his thought chronologically I will limit myself to the most relevant texts.

In 1 Cor 2:6-10 Paul recognizes that the Christian "gnosis" contains a "wisdom." But this wisdom is not the key to the cosmological interpretation of the world. That belongs to what today we could call phenomenology or even philosophy. Paul does not take sides. Christian "wisdom" is a "wisdom of God in mystery." It refers to a design God has on the outcome of history.

This "design" of God or "mystery" is something hidden in God's mind. It had, however, already existed before the existential

---

[4]R. Martin-Archard, *Israel et les Nations*, Neuchâtel-Paris, 1959, p. 66.

development of the different stages or "*eons*" of history, and its climax will coincide with the fulness of human existence: "the wisdom of God in a mystery which was hidden but which God had decreed before the ages for our glorification." This divine decree that moves history in a given direction cannot be known except by positive revelation. This is why "the rulers of this historical situation" will crucify "the Lord of glory." They did not have the key to the "mysterious" reading of history and could not understand that deicide would become the source of mankind's salvation.

Though hidden from them, the "mystery" has been revealed to the prophets through the spirit. "But as it is written, 'no eye has seen, nor ear heard, nor the heart of man conceived, what God has prepared for those who love him,' God has revealed to us through the Spirit."

The "mystery" is not something disassociated from life and separated from the normal and progressive evolution of history. In the following chapter the apostle speaks of "planting" and of "building up." This process of germination and progressive construction will continue until the end of history. Then there will be a divine judgment that will be like fire. And as fire attacking a building makes known the strength of the materials, so also the divine judgment will make known the real contribution of each person toward the maturing task of the world. Perhaps there will be a constructor of good faith who utilized unsuitable materials such as sand and straw. He will be saved, through his good faith, but "through fire" (1 Cor 2:15), that is, like the person who succeeds in coming through the flames of a burning building and barely saves his life leaving behind the ashes of a useless work.

The epistle to the Romans ends with a doxology in which Paul sums this up and carries it to a greater technical precision: "Glory be to God who is able to strengthen you in accordance with the Good News I preach, which heralds the Messiah. This preaching reveals the mystery which has been kept hidden through eternal ages, but, which is now made known by the prophetical writings and proclaimed, by the command of the eternal God, to the Gentiles, so as to bring about the submission to the faith. Yes, to God, who alone is wise, be glory through Jesus Christ for ever and ever. Amen" (Rom 16:25–27).

Here Paul insists on the transcendence of the mystery which in

previous stages of history had not been made manifest. The mystery
is neither more nor less than the Gospel: the official proclamation
of an ancient secret of God. And what is this ancient secret of
God all about? Evidently, its content is the essence of the apostolic
kerygma, especially as Paul has been presenting it throughout the
epistle. We could summarize the content of Paul's gospel extract-
ing it from the great epistle.

Abraham is the great model of the believer. He and Sarah were
sexually as good as dead when God promised them that they would
be the parents of a privileged nation. They recognized their impotence and relied on the power of God, "of a God who gives life
to the dead and calls into existence what was not before." (Rom
4:17) In the same manner believers now recognize their inability
to leap over the abyss of death and "find support in God who raised
Christ from the dead." (4:24) Consequently, Christ's resurrection
is the great event which incorporates the divine "mystery" concerning the success of human existence into the tempo of history.

Hence in chapter 5 Paul draws a parallel between Christ and
Adam. Mankind cannot by itself overcome the fatal effects of
sin and death. It is Christ, the authentic Man, who introduces a
direction toward eternal life into the movement of human evolution. He is the pioneer of those who will be raised up in the future.

The personal work of Christ, however, although it has universal
validity, needs man's collaboration. Paul explains this in chapter
6. True, Christians keep on dying, even after baptism, but through
this baptism they have been integrated into the death of Christ.
No longer do they die their own death, without hope of life.
Instead they die the death of Christ, that is, a death beyond
which there is the certainty of a future victory: the eschatological
resurrection.

We must not think, however, that the Christian is an evasive
man who dreams only of some day liberating himself from the
power of death through a passive expectation of the divine eschatological power. Quite the contrary. In chapter 8, Paul presents man
in total and vital communion with creation, on which hinges the
divine mystery concerning the success of history: "For creation
waits with eager longing for the revealing of the sons of God; for
the creation was subjected to futility, not of its own will but by
the will of him who subjected it in hope; because the creation

itself will be set free from its bondage to decay and obtain the glorious liberty of the children of God. We know that the whole creation has been groaning in travail together until now." (Rom 8:19–22) The "futility" is the uselessness of existence, the lack of meaning. In the narrative of Genesis, chapters one to three, man appears as the meaning given by God to his creative work and he is made responsible for it. He must bring it to successful completion through a work accomplished in dependence on God. It seems that "he who subjected it" is God himself. He made man in a positive manner responsible for creation, and subjected it to the risk of man's freedom. This submission to human destiny, decreed by God, is, however, subject to one "condition": the hope of future liberation. The metaphor taken from the pains of childbirth shows that "the transcendent destiny" given by God to creation is not something discontinuous and prefabricated. It is intimately related to the evolving reality of a world that is gestating another world within itself, a world which will not be totally different but which will supersede the former world in fulness. This is, by way of summary, the content of the "mystery" of God concerning history's destiny. Humanity is rooted in earthly evolution not as a statue upon a pedestal, but as a flower in its bed. When it arrives some day at a successful completion of its existence, it will naturally bring along its own cosmic context, which it cannot do without.

In the epistle to the Galatians, written shortly before the one to the Romans, the apostle had presented at great length the content of the "mystery" in the evolving and progressive aspects which are an integral part of it.

Faithful to the Old Testament concept of salvation through history he interweaves the various successive stages of God's salvific action with the developing internal structure of worldly and human events. This is why he compares the humanity "which must be saved" with the child of a well-to-do family of that time. Mankind did not at first, even though created in the likeness of God, have access to God as a father. Its situation was similar to that of the little child who—despite his being the heir—lived in the slaves' quarters, and in a way that differed little from them. (Gal 4:1–3)

Next, the father "fixes the date" for the child to receive the

toga of the adult and move to the parents' quarters (4:2). The
fixing of the date depended certainly on the free decision of the
father, but up to a point was determined by the child's growth
in years. God, likewise freely established the date of the historical
appearance of Christ (4:4) but it is clearly understood that God
does not prescind from chronological succession. Christ's presence
is not a vertical intervention from above independent of the forward
march of human events. On the contrary, it presumes a given
degree of maturity before which the event cannot occur. Paul
insists on this inescapable dialectic of history. For him it is the
foundation which permits God's salvific action to develop in
step with its own gradual construction. "The law was given until
the offspring could come to whom the promise had been made."
(Gal 3:19) "Before the faith came, we were in the custody of the
law, held captive until the faith should be revealed." (Gal 3:23)
"So the Law was our custodian until Christ came that we may
be sanctified by faith." (Gal 3:24)

In this required chronological succession Paul inserts the event
of Christ's appearance. "When the time had fully come *(to plerōma
tou chronou)* God sent his son, born of a woman, born under the
Law." (Gal 4:4)

Christ's appearance, however, and mankind's subsequent ennoblement do not yet constitute the final stage. It is true that the
Christian is already a son, but he is *still* an heir. (Gal 4:5–7)

In brief, human fulness even though totally dependent upon the
salvific judgment of God is at the same time the final term of
an historical maturing which follows its own rhythm.

In the epistles to the Colossians and to the Ephesians, the
"mystery" acquires a more technical terminology and it is described
in a different way: it is the mystery of the gospel (Eph 6:19):
"The mystery which has been hidden from eternity in God, who
created all things" (Eph 3:9). With this Paul wants to show that
the divine secret refers to God's creative work. It is not something
parallel to or superimposed on creation, but the key, so to speak,
to creation itself.

Specifically, this mysterious key to creation is the Christ event.
Christ is the first born of every creature, "for in him all things
were created in heaven and on earth, visible and invisible, whether

Thrones, or Dominions, or Principalities, or Powers. They all were
created through him and for him." (Col 1:15–16)

This "decree" or divine mystery referring to Christ is something
that must be progressively achieved. In Ephesians the expression
"to fulfill everything" is encountered a number of times: "He fills
all in all." (Eph 1:23) "He who descended is the same one who
has ascended above all the heavens, that he might fully impart
all graces." (Eph 4:10)

But it is in Ephesians 1:9–10 that the "mystery" appears un-
equivocally and explicitly in its historical, on-going function. "God
has made known to us in all wisdom and insight the whole mystery
of his will." Its content is formulated "as a plan he had made beforehand for the fulness of time, to unite all things in him, things in
heaven and things on earth."

"Plan" means here "a fulfillment ordered according to a harmonious design." The "times" or *kairoi* are the different stages
of history previously ordered by God. The fullness of these *kairoi*
is clearly their eschatological consummation. The divine secret is
concentrated in the final point of the harmonious design that God
is producing in history. Irenaeus, so near to the apostle and so
close to his mind, interprets our text simply. He summarizes the
essential points of the Christian creed which (he proclaims) the
Church received from the apostles and disciples. Among the articles
of faith he includes: "the coming of Christ from heaven in the
glory of the Father, to unite all things and to raise all human flesh
from the dead."[5]

Irenaeus himself interprets this "unification" as the final maturing
of a long historical process which must of its nature be evolutionary.
"If anyone asks: could not God have made man perfect?, let him
remember that God is immutable, uncreated, and that as far as
he is concerned, all things are possible. But concerning created
beings, since they have a beginning, they must be inferior to their
creator. They could not be uncreated, for they have recently been
made. And precisely because they are not uncreated, they lack
perfection. Because they are posterior in time, they are as children.
And as children, they are still unaccustomed to and inexperienced

---

[5] Irenaeus, *Against Heretics*, I, 10, 1.

in perfect discipline. A mother cannot feed her child perfectly, since he cannot yet take solid food. Likewise God could have offered man perfection from the very beginning, but man could not have taken it. He was still really a child. And precisely because of this Our Lord came in these last days uniting all things in Himself, not as an expression of the fulness of his power but of the fulness of our ability to see him. He could have come in his ineffable glory, but we would not have been able to stand its grandeur. By this order, this convenience, and this action, created man has been established in the likeness of an uncreated God. This is the will and wish of the Father, the work and creation of the Son, and the food and increment of the Spirit: man's progressive advancement and his access to perfection, that is, God. Man had to be created first. Once created, he had to reach a certain maturity. Once mature, he had to be strengthened. Once strengthened, he would be glorified. Finally, once glorified, he would see his Lord."[6]

From this brief survey of the pauline thought we deduce that "mystery" will never enter into competition with science. "The mystery," says Lacroix, "is neither within science nor touching on its limits. Rather it exists for the man who faces the world with an attitude other than scientific. Science does not suppress art, and there is no art without contemplation. Why would it suppress the religious attitude?"[7] There is a grave danger in any attempt to reduce mystery to cosmological dimensions. It is a kind of sacrilege to appeal to mystery in order to fill the empty spots inevitably left by our imperfect and evolving science.

Science can tranquilly follow its own road without having to clash with mystery. The difference between them is that science seeks explanations of things while mystery seeks their meaning. Such meaning, however, is not purely contemplative, but dynamic. Mystery, as we have just seen in Paul, refers to a plan that God has for the world, considering it precisely in its continuing evolution. The apostles, as ministers, are not simply solemn contemplatives or proclaimers of the mystery but they are explicitly called "stewards of the mysteries of God." (1 Cor 4:1)

It is true that mystery can only be known through positive revela-

[6]Irenaeus, *op. cit.*, IV, 38.
[7]Jean Lacroix, *Histoire et Mystère*, Tournai, 1962, p. 105.

tion. It is something that totally transcends the data of science, but it does not in any way suppress science or make it useless. Mystery is not a short cut to the same destination. It is not an airplane that replaces the uncomfortable stagecoach of science. Mystery has to adapt itself, so to speak, to the evolutionary reality of things. It has to run parallel to the progress of science.

At the same time, this running parallel with science is not purely interpretative, but factual. Mystery does not only mean something. It gradually brings into being what it means. The mystery of God is literally the great sacrament of the world: the key to the divine interpretation of the world and the power to carry it out.

The risen Christ is the essential content of the mystery. He is the man who has achieved his fullness. And his existential fullness is not only a sign in whose light we will be able to perceive the very end to which the divine design destines us, but an initial or primordial power that, having been sowed deep in the evolutionary reality, slowly produces what it signifies. For this reason Baptism is the first sacrament. It is the vital connection with mystery. Man becomes effectively linked with Christ as the resurrectional seed.

From this panoramic view of the pauline theology of mystery we conclude that we must distinguish carefully between the relationship of the individual with the fact of his final salvation and the objective process of salvation itself. Salvation is not an evasion on the part of the individual human being, who has turned his back on the evolutionary happening of history. Salvation is, on the contrary, the final term of the whole slow and progressive movement directly begun by God in the six active days of creation, and continued later by man, in dependence on God during the long day of the creator's sabbatical leave.

This salvation cannot be realized through time saving procedures, independent of the inevitable progressions and development in time of the worldly happening. Even the fact of Christ's appearance could occur only at a given moment of maturity or historical fullness. "When the times had fully come, God sent his son, born of woman, born under the Law." (Gal 4:4)

The men of "good faith" who have lived throughout history will not be excluded from this final entrance into the region of salvation. But a simple attitude on their part of non-rebellion to their own conscience is not enough to make history mature in the "mysterious" sense of the divine plan. True, they lived and died in grace, and for this reason they will not be "condemned." But that grace is not "sufficient" to fulfill history in an effectively salvific sense.

The sacramental grace of mystery is, therefore, necessary. To use a popular comparison, we could say that the men of good faith have died with a ticket to the great stadium of the kingdom of God. But it is necessary to have the stadium really built first. The cornerstone, the "foundation" of the great heavenly stadium, is precisely the risen Christ. M. Feuillet is right in interpreting "the heavenly house" mentioned by Paul in 2 Cor 5.2 as the glorious body of Christ, but as a first fruit of the new creation, that is, insofar as it includes virtually the glorious body of all Christians.[8]

The Church, solely responsible for the realization of the "mystery" of salvation

At this point we relate this directly to our specific question, namely, the mission of the Church with regard to salvation. We have seen that outside the Church the relating of the individual to his final salvation *de facto* takes place. But the eschatological reality of salvation will not really take place without the positive action of the Church.

The Risen Christ is the cornerstone of the great metahistorical stadium of the Kingdom of God. The answer accordingly is that it is the function of the Church to build upon this foundation in order to finish the building in the course of history. The Church is the sacrament of history. Only within the Church is this sacramental or mysterious grace realized. As it is injected into the evolutionary process of humanity, this grace incarnates in the Church in an effective and dynamic manner God's mystery, the divine plan of the successful completion of human and worldly existence.

In his capacity as a great Church leader, Paul was vividly aware of his sacramental responsibility for the developing rhythm of history. Writing to the Romans, he proclaimed that "the grace or apostolic function given him by God" was precisely that of being "a public minister of Christ Jesus to the Gentiles, in the

[8]M. Feuillet, *La Demeure céleste et la destinée de Chrétiens, Recherches de Sciences Religieuses*, 1956, pp. 161–192.

priestly service of the gospel of God, so that the offering of the Gentiles may be acceptable, sanctified by the Holy Spirit." (Rom 15:15) His condition of *leitourgos*, "minister," and of *hierorgounta*, "sanctifier," refers precisely to the fact of the proclamation and establishment among the Gentiles of the Good News of Christ's resurrection. The action of the Church in the world is liturgical and sacramental. It is not the anarchic action of some lone snipers, spreading the message on their own. It is the communal celebration of a unique and peerless rite: the gospel rite.

The celebration of this rite has to take place in every area where there is human life. This was Paul's missionary urgency as opposed to a preoccupation with the "individual salvation" which he so often considered as taken care of by reason of the good faith of a healthy conscience. That was why, immediately after the above mentioned declaration to the Romans, he proceeded to disclose that the specific purpose of his letter was to announce a new phase of operations in his missionary activity: "with mighty signs and wonders, by the power of the Holy Spirit, so that from Jerusalem, and that in all directions, as far as Illyricum, I have fully preached the gospel of Christ. But I have made it a point of honor not to preach the gospel where Christ had already been proclaimed." (Rom 15:19–20) Obviously Paul does not claim that the gospel has already been accepted by every individual in those areas. His main objective was always to leave in every region an established Christian community—large or small—that would make the mystery of God present and operative in the midst of mankind. This explains why he can assert that he no longer has any "further field of action in these parts." (Rom 15:23) This makes him use Rome as the base of operations for further spreading the gospel rite. From the capital of the world he will proceed to the "western end," that is, the Iberian peninsula.

But it is in Ephesians 3:1–12 that Paul formulates with full clarity the mysterious mission of the Church: "I, Paul, a prisoner for the cause of Christ, on behalf of you Gentiles—assuming that you have heard of the stewardship of God's grace that was given to me for you, how the mystery was made known to me by revelation, as I have written briefly. If you read this you can perceive my insight into the mystery of Christ, which was not made known to the sons of men in other generations as it has now been revealed

by the Spirit to his holy apostles and spokesmen; the mystery is
this, that the Gentiles are joint heirs, members of the same body,
and partakers of the promise in Christ Jesus through the gospel.
Of this gospel I was made a minister by the gift of God's grace
which was given me by the working of his power. To me, the
very least of all the saints, this grace was given to preach to the
Gentiles the unsearchable riches of Christ, and to make all men
see what is the plan of the mystery hidden for ages in God who
created all things; that *through the church* the manifold wisdom
of God might now be made known to the principalities and powers
in the heavenly places. This was according to the eternal purpose
which he has realized in Christ Jesus our Lord, in whom we have
assurance and confidence of access through our faith in him."

The fact that the Church is the mediatrix of the "interpretation
of the mystery" presupposes that she is also commissioned to
execute that divine plan throughout the course of history. This
monopoly of the mysterious or sacramental function, reserved to
the Church, is likewise made explicit in the numerous texts of
Colossians and Ephesians in which the Church is presented as
bride, body and *plerōma* (fullness) of Christ. The Church was
already described as bride of Christ in 2 Corinthians, 11:2–3. "I
feel a divine jealousy for you. For I betrothed you, to one spouse
that I might present you a chaste virgin to Christ. But I fear lest,
as the serpent deceived Eve by his cunning, so your thoughts will
be led astray from a sincere and pure devotion to Christ." Here
the Church appears as bride of Christ, recalling the context of the
Genesis narrative of the first human couple, Adam and Eve.

This Genesis background reappears in chapter 5 of the letter
to the Ephesians. The Church is shown as Christ's bride and as
a second Eve. As such she will have a total devotion to her hus-
band. Paul does not say explicitly that next to Christ—the second
Adam—is the Church—the second Eve—but that is what he means.
The comparison implies the monopoly of transmission of biological
power from the male.

This monopoly of "mysterious" fertility granted to the Church
is stressed in the great typology of Galatians 4:21–31. The Church
is compared with Sarah, Abraham's only wife, on whose offspring
the admission into the salvation rhythm of history depended.

In short, the Church is the bride of Christ because only in

her does Christ deposit this resurrectional seed that starts humanity off in its motion toward the successful completion foreseen and signified by the divine mystery.

The Church as the body of Christ has a special nuance in the epistles to the Colossians and the Ephesians. As the head, where according to the biology of the time all the vital centers were located, needs the body as the necessary and exclusive instrument for spreading those vital energies, so also Christ "head of all things" needs the instrumental action of the Church to carry out his sacramental penetration into the evolutionary happening of human history. (Col 1:19; 2:19; Eph 1:23; 4:12; 5:23)

Finally in a sense totally analogous to the two previous expressions, the Church is shown as the *pleroma* of Christ. (Eph 1:22–23; 4:12–13) "Pleroma" has a twofold sense: passive and active. It is passive insofar as it receives from someone else, and active because it shares with others what it receives. In both cases an exclusive distribution is stressed. In this sense, the Church is the "*pleroma* of him who fills (*tou pleroumenou*) all in all." (Eph 1:23) Christ fills all things but not directly. He has his fullness, his *pleroma*, in the Church, in which he deposits all his salvific energy, to irradiate it from there over all the cosmos.

The missionary urgency of the Church governed by mystery

After this concise survey of pauline ecclesiology we can come down to concrete positions regarding the great problem of missionary urgency.

To present as the only motive for the missionary expansion of the Church "the condemnation of souls" in the individual sense we have just examined, would be to falsify the true vision of pauline missiology. Salvation is not the "ticket" for the inauguration of the kingdom of God, but the slow and progressive construction of the Kingdom, which somehow will emerge from this historical situation.

This relation of continuity between history and the kingdom of God has been vividly expressed by Paul: "The whole creation is pregnant with the kingdom of God." It belongs to the Church to be the midwife in the sublime function of bringing to life the future of history, according to the mystery of God.

The Church has no reason to make up her own history as something marginal to the real events of the world. There is no history of salvation parallel or counter to universal history. The Church owns the key to the interpretation and transformation of the only history there is. For that reason she welcomes the evolutionary reality that is offered to her. What is called rather ambiguously "natural right" is something the Church does not create. She presupposes it. She is to "serve" all the institutions that in a positive manner authentically promote humanity. This revelation does not create anew a total system of human relations, civilizations, and cultures.

Outside the ecclesial realm there are many things that are acceptable, prior to, and independent of the Church. The task of the latter is only to be able to read carefully the divine mystery hidden in those realities, to proclaim their interpretation, and to act according to the significance of the same mystery.

For this reason we cannot speak of a Christian humanism. The Church cannot be reduced to any concrete form of humanism, making it her own as the only Christian possibility. The only dialectical alternative we find in the activity of the Church is virtue and sin, or more specifically, love and selfishness. Outside these, all differences and all alternatives are possible in the liturgical celebration of the gospel rite: "There is no Greek or Jew, circumcised or uncircumcised, no free man or slave, but only and in every thing Christ."

The missionary urgency that so forcefully impelled Paul was governed by this "mysterious" sense of history which the Church is monopolistically supposed to insert in the evolutionary reality of the development of the world.

This mysterious sense of history, therefore, refers basically to the conscious and personalized unity of humanity. Humanity needs to be tightly united despite its great diversity. This world will not be mature enough to go through the barrier of time and to leap into eternity unless a planetary unity has been achieved.

This unity must be totally "personal," realized in the maximum expansion of conscience and free decision. For this reason, the Church must oppose on the one hand everything that separates mankind, and on the other hand everything that threatens to make it a totalitarian unity, realized at the price of the brutal sacrifice of the free expansion of personality.

Now we understand why the mission of the Church is precisely to preach and to spread love for the neighbor. This is her secret, her true mystery. The constitution of Christian communities all over the world has no purpose other than to multiply examples of the great and exclusive product of the Church: love for the neighbor.

E. Schillebeeckx in his book *Christ, Sacrament of the Encounter with God* expresses this idea as follows: "It is necessary for the Church's holiness to become truly visible to all men. In this, it seems to me, we find the main crisis facing its present-day apostolate. Very many indeed have wearied of the Church precisely because its outward appearance is so disappointing. We find signs of this at a very early stage in its history. St. Augustine himself complained . . . those who had already come close to me on the way to believing . . . are frightened away far too often by the bad lives of evil and false Christians. How many, my brothers, do you think there are who want to become Christians, but are put off by the evil ways of Christians? (*Enarrationes in Psalmos*, ps. 30, sermo 2, 6) It is symptomatic that in the Western World, in which the Church has been rooted for centuries, the mass of the people no longer see or hear its witness. It is so easy simply to pass Christianity by. Hence in one way or another the witness, the telling visibility of the grace of Christ is kept hidden. Yet it cannot be said that the level of the Church's holiness has fallen. There are, therefore, only two possible explanations: Either human encounter is no longer made use of as the effective sacrament of our love of God, and Christians sanctify themselves in their own little corner without having any contact with the rest of the world, or where new methods of approach in apostolic work have re-established a living contact with men, this human encounter is not sufficiently an interpretation of an inward encounter with God, a sacrament of divine love, but merely a new kind of convert propaganda. It seems to me that both explanations are valid. To develop an awareness and an appreciation of the fact that the power of appeal in Christianity lies in the visible presence of grace, in the sense just explained, is not simply another tactic, a new method of apostolate, but demands a real and unfeigned love of neighbour. To use this order of things as a technical method of religious efficiency would be to degrade holiness to the level of a means of propaganda. This would destroy genuine holiness and therefore the power of attraction in the visible presence of grace. In our times we cannot recommend higher values to people by making speeches about them. People—to put it very bluntly—have had their bellyful of our sermonizing. They are seeking a source of strength for their lives; they want a sense and a meaning that will give them this strength. The higher values and vital strength can be recommended to others only by making them actively present in ourselves. Contact with Christians must be an experience which proves to men that Christianity is a power transforming the whole life."[9]

The last events of the pontificate of John XXIII and those of the beginning of Paul VI offer us the start of an authentic re-evangelization of the world in planetary dimensions. The Church has been exposed to everyone as a "sign raised before the people," as a sacrament of brotherly love in history. Missionary urgency compels the best and most generous Christians throughout the world to multiply authentic Christian communities that would again be called "communities of love" (*agape*) as the first Christian generation (and Paul himself) used to call their communities.

Therefore, when missionaries go to pagan countries they go precisely to build "Church" in the most literal sense of the expression. The presence of the true Church of love among all races has to become a gentle invitation to the world in whose midst she lives. The Church cannot look down upon the world or fail to acknowledge and accept its values. Despite her firm position of *magisterium*, she must begin by assuming the attitude of a disciple trying to accept and enrich herself with all the positive realities of the atmosphere in which she develops. Her preaching has to be "not in persuasive words of 'wisdom,' but in demonstrations of the Spirit's power." (1 Cor 2:4) And these demonstrations are what in a "cordially inviting manner," as Paul VI put it in his coronation message, will bring about the authentic conversion of men, according to the dream of the prophet Zechariah: "Thus says the Lord of hosts: in those days, ten men of all nations of every tongue shall take hold of the robe of a Jew saying: let us go with you, for we have heard that God is with you." (Zec 8:23)

[9]E. Schillebeeckx, *Christ, the Sacrament of the Encounter with God*, Sheed and Ward, New York, 1963, p. 207–8.

Only in this way will the Church be able to accomplish her unifying task of bringing men together with God and with themselves—a necessary task if human history is to acquire the maturity demanded for its transtemporal transition to eternity.

The Church is truly responsible for history. The divine mystery of redemption rests on humanity of all ages: the happy destiny of all men and of all things. The Church is the only one assigned to interpret this mystery and to develop its dynamism within the evolutionary thrust of the world as it moves forward toward its destiny.

To sum up, the Mission belongs to the very essence of the ecclesial task: the missionary urgency is intrinsically governed by the mysterious and sacramental sense of history.

CHAPTER 9

THE PEOPLE OF GOD

The second chapter of the Dogmatic Constitution of the Church is entitled "The People of God." We will not devote any time to the background of this ecclesial title either in its deep biblical roots or in its recent incorporation into Catholic ecclesiology. We will limit ourselves to outlining this second chapter of the Conciliar Constitution, stressing the enormous advance that the integration of this title presupposes for the theology of the Church, especially with regard to her "worldly" projection. We will therefore follow the thread of the conciliar text itself, pointing out the meaningful definitions it contains, definitions which are bound to condition radically the new ecclesiological treatises.

People

The Chapter begins with the words: "At all times and in every nation God has given welcome to whoever fears him and does what is right. It has pleased God, however, to make men holy and save them not merely as individuals without any mutual bonds; rather has it pleased him to make of them a People . . ."[1]

This is simply an authoritative interpretation of the old theological slogan "*Extra ecclesiam nulla salus.*" This axiom has been the cause of great confusion, because of failure to distinguish what I would call "individual salvation" from "ecclesial salvation."

Throughout the Bible we can detect a constant imbalance between

[1] Dogmatic Constitution on the Church, *The Teachings of the Second Vatican Council*, Newman Press, p. 82.

God's justice and his mercy, in favor of the latter. God does not condemn anyone except after a long and conscious rebellion. "The Lord has no pleasure in the death of the wicked, and he would rather that he should turn from his way and live." (Ez 18:23) "God wills that all men be saved and come to the knowledge of the truth." (1 Tim 2:4) If this is so, how are we to explain the constant insistence of the New Testament on presenting the Church as the only instrument of salvation for humanity?

As we shall see in other passages of the chapter on which we are commenting, salvation in the Bible is a historical-communal concept. God has not created men as isolated and independent individuals, but as a unity. According to the platonic concept generation was a mere occasion for the multiplication of human spirits. The body—and the world—was nothing but the vessel of the spirit, acting as cage or cell, or in the best of cases, as a rehearsal stage for the pure virtuosity of the spirit.

In the Bible, on the contrary, man is the whole composite of his existence with a heavy emphasis on his corporeal dimension and his insertion in the cosmic context.

According to Plato, "salvation" consists in the liberation of the spirit from the corporeal vessel and its cosmic context. In the biblical concept "salvation" includes essentially and primarily the rehabilitation of the body and its final establishment in the renewed cosmos.

This antithetic notion of salvation reaches a climax when the hitherto-unheard-of Christian message based on faith in the resurrection breaks into the old Greek society. The following text from the first letter to the Corinthians is an exceptional document on the great contrast between both conceptions: "Now if Christ is preached as raised from the dead, how is it that some of you say there is no resurrection from the dead? If there is no resurrection from the dead, Christ was not raised. . . . If Christ has not been raised, your faith is groundless; you are still in your sins! . . . If for this life only we have hoped in Christ, we are more to be pitied than all other men. But Christ has truly been raised from the dead, the first fruit of those who have fallen asleep. . . . If the dead are not raised at all, why am I in peril every hour? What do I gain if from human motives I fought wild beasts at Ephesus, what use was it to me? If the dead are not raised, 'Let us eat and drink, for tomorrow we die.' " (1 Cor 15:12–13, 17, 19–20; 29c–30a, 32)

This language as we can see is in complete contrast to that employed by Hellenic soteriology. Salvation, for Christianity, includes as an essential element victory over corporeal death. For this reason, the event of Christ's resurrection is the center of our faith. It is the guarantee and first fruit of the resurrection of men on the frontiers of their own history.

This essentially material salvation is placed at the end of the long process of the human adventure, and it also encompasses the cosmic context itself where the whole internal structure of history is developed. Paul refers explicitly to this in chapter 8 of his letter to the Romans: "I consider the sufferings of this present time as not worthy to be compared with the glory to come. All creation awaits with eager longing the revealing of the sons of God; for creation was subjected to futility, not of its own choice but by the will of him who subjected it in hope; because the creation itself will be set free from its bondage to decay and obtain the glorious liberty of the children of God. We know that all creation groans and travails in pain until now; and not only the creation, but we ourselves, who have the first fruit of the spirit, groan inwardly as we wait for adoption as sons, the redemption of our bodies." (Rom 8:18–23)

According to this exclusively Christian conception, salvation in the full meaning of the term is something of the future, to occur only at the end of human history, when in the *parousia* of Christ all the dead will rise and the kingdom of God will be inaugurated.

What happens to each individual after his own death has an essential connection with this salvation, but it cannot yet be called "salvation" in a strict theological sense.

According to this biblical conception we should distinguish between salvation in the wide sense and salvation in the strict sense.

In the wide sense, salvation can be understood as a final judgment of God on the behavior of each human being, passed at the time of death. If this sentence is favorable, this man is basically saved, although his "salvation" is still at an impasse waiting for the definitive situation which will take place only at the end of history and which will have to be shared by the collectivity of all saved human beings. In the strict sense salvation is eschatological and communal. It is a fact that has not taken place yet, and will be effected only when the human adventure really comes to a conclusion. In this sense salvation is a future event that somehow has to develop and mature gradually in the midst of an ever progressive human history.

The people of God—the Church—has therefore been summoned so that this maturing can be attained at the heart of history itself. The Dogmatic Constitution uses a very well chosen formula which translates this biblical vision of the people of God in the world into modern language: *"In historiam hominum intrat."* (It enters the history of men.)

The presence of the people of God in time and space is therefore intended not only to offer each individual the richness of its spiritual goods. Very importantly, in addition, it seeks to introduce a parousial rhythm into the ongoing trend of human history itself, a rhythm which eventually will cause it to flow into the kingdom of God.

The slogan *extra ecclesiam nulla salus* should not be understood about salvation in the wide sense. As the Constitution explicitly admits, God does not refuse this salvation to anyone of good will. It must, however, be understood of salvation in the strict sense. Without the presence of the people of God throughout history, humanity will end up in failure. In other words, it will not reach the meta-historical situation of the kingdom of God.

In this respect the Constitution makes two important affirmations: 1.) "Those also can attain to salvation who through no fault of their own do not know the gospel of Christ or his Church, yet sincerely seek God and moved by grace strive by their deeds to do his will as it is known to them through the dictates of conscience."[2]

2.) "Whosoever, . . . knowing that the Catholic Church was made necessary by Christ, would refuse to enter it or to remain in it, could not be saved."[3]

Paul was fully aware of the fact that the mission of the Church is not fulfilled by seeking only the "individual salvation" which is available to all men of good faith. Rather it essentially involves her presence in the human family, thereby creating in it the impact

[2]Constitution on the Church, no. 16, *op. cit.*, p. 94.
[3]Constitution on the Church, no. 14, *op. cit.*, p. 92.

of unity that only love for one's neighbor, preached and practiced by Christians, can effectively produce. This is why he writes to the Romans, referring to the numerous churches founded by him along the eastern shore of the Mediterranean: "Now I no longer find any room for work in these regions." (Rom 10:23) He knew very well that not by any means had all individuals joined the Christian communities of Asia Minor and Greece. He nevertheless considered his mission as finished after having achieved the presence of those small ecclesial seeds in the vast extension of the Mediterranean. Now he wants to bring the gospel to the western shores, to Spain and he accordingly envisions Rome as the new general headquarters for the escalating evangelization.

In brief, the concept and expression of "people" applied to the Church stresses the communal and parousial character of salvation as contrasted with the wide and individual sense which strictly speaking would not demand the presence of the Church as a necessary element of salvation.

This is the only valid starting point for a theology of the missions.

In the world and for the world

The dogmatic constitution has a perfectly internal consistence. The concept of the people of God as responsible from within for the parousial rhythm of history finds its perfect explanation in this concise formula: "So it is that that messianic people, although it does not actually include all men, and at times may look like a small flock, is nonetheless a lasting and sure seed of unity, hope and salvation for the whole human race."[4] Although the Church holds her doors open for everybody and constantly attempts to widen her frontiers, very often she will be a minority within the immense masses of humanity. Her mission is not limited to proselytizing, to increasing the number of her members. Even when in a minority situation, she is still a salvific seed in the midst of human society. The Christian Church appeared in the midst of the historical world of religions as a total break with self-contentment. The community of believers in Christ did not try to find an extra-territorial oasis where they could set up for themselves their own culture, their own history, their own language. On the contrary,

[4]Constitution on the Church, no. 9, op. cit., p. 83–84.

they are to be found immersed in and dispersed among the people and society.

As a "community," the first obvious step is to undertake a process of "ecclesialization." *Ekklesia* means precisely the fact of coming together, and not the community resulting from it. In the first Christian generation the process of ecclesialization was conceived strictly as an instrument to effect the "worldification" of Christians to enable them to be in the world like the others. In the second century a Christian author describes as follows the worldly modes of the believers of his community: "Christians are no different from other men, either by their region or by their language, or by their customs. Each one lives in his own country, even though as a pilgrim. They participate in everything like every other citizen, and they bear everything like foreigners. A foreign land is for them like their homeland, and their homeland like a foreign land. They marry like every one else, they procreate, but they do not indulge in abortion. They have a common table, but not a common bed. . . . They obey the law, but with their own resources they go beyond their law. . . . In brief, Christians are for the world what the soul is for the body."[5]

Christians, in other words, are here not to create their own world but to insert themselves into the world, offering the service of a morality governed by brotherly love.

The communities founded by Paul already experienced a temptation to disregard the process of worldification and limit themselves to a simple ecclesialization, that is, an ecclesial inflation. In Philippi, the first European community, an "integralist" group attempted to introduce Christianity by totally erasing the previous religious experience. The effort was aimed specifically at the Stoic morality, and it resulted in a division in the community. The integralists believed that the Church had a complete autonomy and that she alone was capable of segregating the moral values of the spirit. For this reason even the noble Stoic morality had to be done away with. Paul roundly condemns this narcissist attitude of the integralists: "Whatever is true, whatever is honorable, whatever just, whatever pure, whatever lovable, whatever merits praise, if there is any excellence, if there is anything worthy of praise, such

[5]Epis. ad Diog. M6z, 11773.

are the things you should keep in mind." (Phil 4:8) The terminology employed by Paul is clearly taken from the Stoic morality. In Corinth there were several groups or *ekklesiai* that would convene regularly to celebrate the Eucharist. When a new convert approached Christians the temptation of ecclesial inflation was easily felt. In consequence, if the ecclesial group he approached was predominantly Jewish and he was a Greek, he would take it on himself to look for another *ekklesia* where Greeks would constitute the majority. The same would happen with slaves and free men. Paul reacted strongly against this discrimination. Each one, he insisted, must remain in the ecclesial gathering to which the call to Christianity brought him, even though that *ekklesia* may not correspond to his cultural, technical, or social background. (1 Cor 7:17–24)

This dialectical tension between ecclesialization and worldification is one of the main points emphasized in the second chapter of the Dogmatic Constitution on the Church. Ecclesialization is not an end in itself. It is subordinated to worldification. The People of God "is used by Christ as an instrument for the redemption of all, and is sent forth into the whole world as the light of the world and the salt of the earth."[6] A process of ecclesialization that totally absorbs the biological forces of the Church keeping her from going to the world outside, from living in it, from breathing its air, from assimilating its values, is undoubtedly a serious attempt on this essential dimension of the People of God, "universal instrument of redemption, light of the world, and salt of the earth."

This pathology of introversion is felt in many areas of ecclesial life: theology becomes abstract, nominalist, and angelist; morality gets lost in insignificant casuistic *minutiae*; religious life is reduced to conventual patterns; preaching loses the vigor required for an authentic prophetic denunciation.

As a consequence of it all, the Church eclipses the sacramental transparency of its essential condition of "sign." The Constitution says that the Church must be a "seed of unity, hope and salvation" in the midst of the world. How the Church must perform this germinal mission in the world is explained by the Constitution's stress on the prophetic dimension of the People of God.

[6]Constitution on the Church, no. 9, *op. cit.*, p. 84.

Prophetic dimension of the People of God

"The holy People of God," says the council, "shares also in Christ's prophetic office; it spreads abroad a living witness to Him, especially by means of a life of faith and charity and by offering to God a sacrifice of praise, the tribute of lips which give praise to His name."[7]

In the Old Testament there were two functions—priestly and prophetic—exercised by different persons. The priest was only the man of the cult. The preaching of the message of God was entrusted to the prophet. But in the New Testament the two functions have been unified and are exercised by the same person and by one institution. The priesthood of the New Testament belongs to the whole Church. Nevertheless, the Constitution distinguishes a common priesthood—that is to say, a priesthood of the faithful—and a ministerial priesthood. These are essentially different from each other yet intimately connected. In any case, the Church is a priestly people, which joins in herself the twofold function—priestly and prophetic—of the two institutions of the Old Testament.

Here again we find the need to look for a dialectical equilibrium between the two dimensions. At times the priestly role has largely replaced the prophetic one, and then the Church has appeared not as a sign of love and faith, but as a sign of hieratic magnificence. The ministerial priesthood itself has grown toward an ever greater similarity to the strict priesthood of the Old Testament, thus losing the heights of its prophetic grandeur. The absorption of the prophetic by the cultual has immediate consequences in the attitude of the Church toward the world. Now that Vatican II has struggled to readjust the equilibrium between the two functions with the help of the Constitution on the Church in the Modern World, one can understand the painful crisis that pastors and laymen are going through when an effort is made to determine the extent and content of a strictly ecclesial activity, such as apostolic activity. Nevertheless a reconsideration of the essential nature of the prophetic role within the priestly ministry of the Church is absolutely necessary in order to reach a way of living and acting

[7]Constitution on the Church, no. 12, op. cit., p. 88.

consistent with the prophetic dimensions of the People of God, so clearly stressed by the Dogmatic Constitution.

To reduce the priestly function—both ministerial and lay—exclusively or primarily to its cultic aspect would narrow the concept of "religion." It would mean an individual mystique and asceticism closer to Plato's concept of salvation than to the biblical vision of man taken in his totality and his insertion in the cosmic context. Were this allowed to happen, ecclesial preaching or evangelization would move on an angelist level. It would proceed on the assumption that the salvation preached by Christ referred only to a part of the human being. The men of the Church would be absent preachers, always calling our attention to an eschatological end, totally discontinuous from and unconnected with the development of human history. "Save your soul" would be the motto of the angelist preacher. He would not be concerned at all with the events of this world: the great social injustices, wars, hunger, oppression, violation of human freedom. It is a position which even the most superficial reading of the Bible makes untenable. In the Old Testament the prophets were men fully informed about the political and economic situation of the country, and in their fervent preaching they made specific reference to it. The prophets did not speak in the abstract. In the name of God they could take concrete sides, in favor of Babylon and against Egypt, in favor of Edom and against the Israelite kingdom of the North. In the gospel we see the bold figure of John the Baptist standing up to the chief of State, King Herod, even to the point of suffering capital punishment. Jesus himself denounces clearly and forcibly the unjust retention of power in the hands of a small exploiting oligarchy: the scribes and pharisees. "Blind leaders, straining out a gnat, and swallowing a camel!" (Mt 23:34) He applies to Herod such a strong expression as "fox." (Lk 13:32) However, it is not clear yet on what principles and to what extent the Church as such—ministerial and lay priesthood—must extend her prophetic function to commit herself in the concrete, political, social, economical or cultural situations. In order to clarify this point the Constitution underlines the total and purely *religious* aspect of the ecclesial society.

Purely religious nature of the Church

"Among all the nations of the earth," remarks the Constitution, "there is but one People of God, which takes its citizens from every nation, making them citizens of a kingdom which is of a heavenly rather than of an earthly nature. For all the faithful, scattered though they be throughout the world, are in communion with each other in the Holy Spirit, so that 'he who occupies the See of Rome knows those afar as his members.' Since the kingdom of Christ is not of this world, the Church or People of God takes nothing away from the temporal welfare of any people. Rather does it foster and adopt, insofar as they are good, the ability, riches, and customs of each people. Taking them to itself it purifies, strengthens, elevates and consecrates them."[8]

As we see, the Dogmatic Constitution gives in the twentieth century the same solution Paul gave to the Christian community of Philippi.

The Church, therefore, cannot pretend to set herself up as a territorial sanctuary endowed with autonomy and with resources of her own. Grace is not here to substitute for the natural sources of human values. It comes only to give them power, to strengthen and ennoble them. The Church has not received from Christ the command to produce political, social, or cultural techniques. This is the task of mankind as such, prior to the establishment of the Church in the midst of human society. Therefore the Church has no reason to create a Christian political doctrine, a Christian culture, a Christian society, a Christian state, not even a Christian party.

The Church, on the other hand, has as its mission to offer the service of the Gospel. And the Gospel will specifically condition the political, social, and economic aspects of the world. For the salvation offered by the Gospel encompasses the whole man in his historical and concrete setting, although with a projection toward his intrahistorical fulfillment. This means that the intervention of the Church in the concrete human situation has to maintain the painful and difficult equilibrium of a dialectical tension. This dialectical tension reaches its climax in the problem of Church-State relations.

In the New Testament the State always appears as something extrinsic to the kerygmatic and soteriological activity exclusively entrusted to the Church. The Church provides the only atmosphere in which the unique lordship of Christ is proclaimed, and from which the gradual establishment of the kingdom of Christ in the midst of an ever progressing history occurs. From this point of view Church

[8]Constitution on the Church, no. 13, op. cit., p. 89–90.

and State relations will maintain a just equilibrium if—and only if—both sides limit themselves to their own functions without interfering with the other's.

The State as such is not an ecclesial setting and can in no way be identified with the People of God. This is the novelty introduced by Christianity as compared with the situation in ancient Israel. If the State as such assumes certain kerygmatic or even soteriological functions, this equilibrium is immediately subjected to grave risks.

Likewise, the Church as such is a purely religious setting, and must not be contaminated with even the appearance of civil power. In this sense we must understand the insistence of the apostolic writers of the New Testament in exhorting Christians to submit to temporal power, so that the Church does not appear as a more or less powerful rival of the State.

When the Church signs a treaty or yields to the temporal power by accepting privileges or exemptions which compromise her and reduce her to the position of a parasite society under the jurisdiction of the State, her "religious freedom" or her capacity of prophetic denunciation of the abuses of the three concupiscences is greatly hampered. And this is the precise moment at which progressive absorption of the prophetic by the cultic takes place as a result of what can be described as a biological selection. An improper equation of the cultic and religious is made, with the result that inflation of the cultic renders the Church really profane by amputating the most essential part of her religious condition: the prophetic role. In brief, the greater the religious purity of the Church, the more efficient will her capacity be to influence the world, as "seed of unity, hope, and salvation."

This Church, fully religious, that is, prophetic, must make concrete and committed decisions in respect of individual and collective human situations. The interesting part is that the ecclesial action must always be an authentic sign of love. The Church is a sacrament of history. Sacrament means that it is the sign of something the sacrament itself produces. The mission of the Church is to produce brotherly love in human relations. Her performance must always be a sign of love. A sign, in order to be such, must be clear and intelligible. If the people en masse interpret the performance of the Church on the temporal level as dictated by ambition, selfishness, power or subjection, she has ceased to be the sign and hence the sacrament of history.

Undoubtedly, in many historical situations, efforts have been made to reduce the Church to the language of cult and liturgy used only inside the temples. Attempts have been made to seal her lips, so that she could no longer emit a prophetic cry of protest, like the prophet Jesus proclaiming happiness for the poor, for the hungry, for the thirsty, for those in prison, Jesus who condemned the rich, the oppressors, the self-satisfied and the overfed. The People of God—the priestly People—must stop at certain crossroads in history to make a serious and probing examination of conscience concerning certain cowardly silences which have definitely eclipsed the sacramental transparency of the Church.

Intrahistorical and transcendent

To carry out its religious-cultic-prophetic mission in the midst of history, the People of God must sustain a new dialectical tension: incarnation-transcendence. The Dogmatic Constitution formulates with precision this difficult position: "While it transcends all limits of time and national boundaries, the Church is destined to extend to all regions of the earth and so enters into the history of mankind."[9]

In this sense, Christianity meant a deep novelty for the two religious worlds in which she was born and developed. Judaism was as such a universal religion. Nevertheless it had provisionally, as Paul put it, linked the possession and preaching of the message with a given people. The racial, cultural, historical, and geographical limits of the Jewish people had become in fact a frontier of the biblical religion itself.

Paganism, on the other hand, was identified with the customs, uses, and topography of the Western world. *Cuius regio eius religio.* There were sacred and profane places for both worlds, sacred and profane meals, sacred and profane persons. Priests formed a group apart which exercised a great influence even in civil life. In Rome Caesar was *Pontifex Maximus*, whereas in Jerusalem the High Priest was *de facto* the national leader of the Jewish people. Jesus' answer: "Render to Caesar what is Caesar's and to God what is God's" (Mt 22:21) totally suppresses the ideological presuppositions of both worlds.

The gospel means surpassing the conception of religion as "ghetto."

[9]Constitution on the Church, no. 9, *op. cit.*, p. 84.

The alternative Jerusalem Gerizim is overcome. (Jn 4:21) Before there was a narcissist concept of religion. That was Judaism. The true religion had hardened and crystallized into a fixed sociological form. Religion had been degraded in culture and civilization. To accept the religion of Yahweh, one had to become "jewish" with all the sociological and cultural implications of such a difficult choice. The great stumbling block introduced by Jesus was that he took apart the whole political-social-religious apparatus in which the old religion of the prophets had been degraded. This "judaizing" temptation will accompany the Church throughout her weary pilgrimage in history. After the Constantinian peace in particular the powerful myth of *sacrum imperium* begins to take shape, and it will dominate the whole activity of the Church during the long medieval period. We are not going to make any simplistic judgment about an era so full of varying events as the Middle Ages, but it is true that little by little a concrete equation between Christianity and Western civilization began to form. The result was Christendom. There was again a people— the people of God—whose frontiers were truly wider than those of the ancient people of Israel and to whom citizenship was granted with a greater and more generous ease than in the Old Testament times. But deep down the "judaizing" situation had reappeared in medieval Christianity. Christian was no longer an adjective but a noun. Once more there were sacred and profane places, sacred and profane persons. Clericalism experienced a period of revival. The pope was not only Peter's successor but, in a certain sense, the successor of the Roman imperial heritage as well. The bishops were not only the successors of the apostles. At times they also performed functions that had belonged to the Roman prefects. Peter's successor was given the old pagan name *Pontifex Maximus* or the Jewish title "High Priest." Kings and even emperors were consecrated by the Popes, and the latter could absolve subjects from obedience due to the emperor or to the king. Christendom had its own frontiers, beyond which were the pagans, God's enemies. The preaching of the Gospel was at times in practice confused with the wish for living space that assails all great empires. Here, in part, is found the justification of the crusades.

The fifteenth century saw the phenomenon of the Renaissance and parallel to it the painful schism of Western Christian unity. The core of the Renaissance rebellion was precisely the desire to shake off a clerical yoke that had proved a heavy burden on the development of human values. It is interesting to observe that the shibboleth of rebellion was always a return, assumed or real, to the Gospel. Christian instinct survived despite the variegated confusion of the papal court and the feudalism of bishops and abbots.

After a moment of uncertainty during the massive separation of great numbers of Christians, the Roman Church attempted to rally her forces and the process of narcissism—from which she is now attempting to liberate herself—began. The Council of Trent was preoccupied with the internal affairs of the Church. The problem of ecclesialization occupied the whole attention of the Church rulers. It must be recognized that it was the only solution to ensure the survival of a Church which was widely corrupted in her most intimate and characteristic elements. In this sense the Council of Trent deserves far more respect and admiration from us than a superficial or snobbish analysis of that great assembly is likely to accord.

From the period of Trent onwards, the Roman Church accepted her reduced status and concentrated on strengthening her own position, a position which was still powerful in relation to the development of Western civil society. Nevertheless, the process of emancipation from clerical power begun by the Renaissance followed its normal process according to a regular dialectic dynamism: the French revolution, the Enlightenment, socialism, communism. The human group that constituted the Catholic Church was still strong and powerful. It was, however, excessively concentrated on itself and full of nostalgia for its lost power. In this situation the Church took on again the aspect of old medieval Christendom, but transferring to the spiritual realm the power then displayed on the temporal (or better yet, temporal-spiritual) level. The Holy Office succeeded the Inquisition, using harsh spiritual weapons against the faithful. After the popes lost their temporal power forever, the diminutive Vatican State was born, and the old splendor of the pontifical court—purified and decanted—was there concentrated.

Finally appeared the disconcerting and unexpected figure of John XXIII followed by Vatican Council II which he convoked and protected. And while it may seem pessimistic to sum up the story of the Church in these terms, it is not really so. A Church that after such hazardous contingencies is capable of gathering in council and carrying out a monumental self-revision without undercutting her foundations, presupposes the continuity of a rich spiritual and evangelical vein flourishing despite everything throughout her entire history.

Popular and lay elements in the Church

Finally, let me mention another of the most happy and most embracing expressions of chapter two of the Dogmatic Constitution on the Church. "The entire body of the faithful, anointed as they are by the Holy One, cannot err in matters of belief. They manifest this special property by means of the whole people's supernatural discernment in matters of faith when 'from the bishops down to the last of the lay faithful' they show universal agreement in matters of faith and morals."[10]

Naturally this infallibility in faith, characteristic of the People of God as such, obliges the teachers and pastors of the Church to listen very carefully to this vital reality of the People. The whole theology of dialogue which is building up at the present time, under the special protection of Pope Paul VI's Encyclical *Ecclesiam Suam*, had its starting point right here. You cannot develop a theology solely from above, without having previously known experimentally the reactions and expressions of that People of God "which has been anointed by the Holy Spirit."

This logically presents the problem of freedom and the stimulus of religious expression within the Church and her institutions.

The search for a religious formulation, like any other human research, entails some risks. But this must not be an obstacle to undertaking the adventure with ever growing enthusiasm. Those who search and research must be willing to recognize humbly the insufficiency and the defects of the tiresome stages involved in their search. And the pastors or guardians of the faith must make their observations and corrections with a paternal affection that will do nothing to discourage the researchers, while inspiring them to continue the search despite the inadequacies of the results.

In this context, far greater stress should be placed on the need to deepen and broaden our efforts in the sphere of religious sociology. The universal sense of the Christian people can be captured by serious sociological investigations which detect and evaluate the human phenomenon in its true and concrete context.

18Constitution on the Church, no. 12, *op. cit.*, p 88.

In modern terminology the gospel command to "know your sheep" must be translated into terms of religious sociology. In this sense it is really hopeful to see a scientific study of theology in the strict sense flourish among laymen, thus following custom which has a long tradition in the oriental Church. The layman belongs more closely to the People of God, insofar as the latter is popular and universal. He will thus be able to bring his theological reflection to all the vital corners of the immense ecclesial body.

The lay theologian will undoubtedly constitute a decisive element in the most urgent task of developing a "theology of the world," especially as regards the "worldly" aspects of ecclesiology itself.

CHAPTER 10

A New "Christendom"?

In his book, *The Death of God*, Gabriel Vahanian criticises Maritain's form of Christian humanism. He argues (a) that it is not deeply Christian, that is, biblical; (b) that, if this Christian humanism constitutes the only possibility of a reincarnation of Christianity in the new civilization, we can look forward to nothing less than a complete failure.

(a) Maritain's "Christian humanism" does not correspond to the biblical conception:

"Maritain stipulates that this new age of Christian civilization must be founded on the distinction between the spiritual and the temporal orders, between religion and culture. This distinction appears to be in agreement with the Biblical view, but the agreement is merely superficial. It conceals a readmission of the classical error of dualism between heaven and earth, body and soul, together with the resultant dichotomous view of religion and culture. Maritain writes that culture is merely concerned with terrestrial matters, but the goals of religion are supraterrestrial and that such a differentiation is 'essential to Christianity.' Any attempt which presents the Christian faith in a mode susceptible to act as a leaven in molding the spirit of the contemporary world yet thwarts or belittles the intrinsic worth and the needs of that spirit is a sign of the inherent weakness of Christianity."[1]

(b) This autonomy of profane culture in face of Christian spirituality leads fatally to a position of disdain for the intrinsic values of civilization:

"Maritain's positive approach to the independent reality of culture

[1] George Braziller, Inc.—from *The Death of God* by Gabriel Vahanian, reprinted with the permission of the publisher. Copyright © 1957, 1959, 1960, 1961 by Gabriel Vahanian.

is but a pretext better to absorb it into the realm of an otherworldly reality, namely the Christian tradition. But he does not thereby salvage it from its increasing irrelevance, for if the artist must endeavor to become a saint, his art is superfluous. As Mauriac has said, if one were a saint, one would not write novels. Nor would one be a doctor, nor a politician nor, to use Maritain's own words, 'anything here below, save perhaps a monk.' . . . All that achieves is to reassert the old deprecation of life here on earth. Maritain, like many another Christian throughout the ages, speaks highly of culture and the arts; he is, even more than many another, concerned about their vitality under a Christian influence; yet his views reveal the same spirit of otherworldliness and contempt for this world on which centuries of Christianity have thrived . . . It is a question, therefore, whether any rethinking of Christianity in contemporary terms can be relevant so long as no simultaneous attempt is made to dislocate and expel the habits of life-denial which have characterized Christianity. The problem is as simple and unambiguous as Marx expressed it: 'It is easy to become a saint of one does not want to be a man.' "[2]

We cannot deny that Maritain has not completely overcome the dualism attributed to him by Vahanian and that he presents it in terms of contrast with the truly integral concept of authentic biblical humanism. Nevertheless, I think Vahanian's negative judgment must be qualified.

In the first place, it must be recognized that Maritain seriously attempts to evaluate man's effort with regard to the eschatological fulfillment of the kingdom of God. "What we have said of this inevitable doublemeaning (ambivalence) of secular history implies that the Christian must needs strive *even harder* to realize in this world (perfectly and absolutely in the case of himself as an individual; in a relative mode and according to the concrete ideal which belongs to each different age with regard to the world itself) the truths of the Gospel. We can never strive hard enough, never be sufficiently devoted to this endeavour to advance the conditions of our terrestrial life and to transfigure it. This state of tension and warfare is a necessary condition of the growth of history, the essential condition whereby the history of time enigmatically prepares its final consummation in the Kingdom of God."[3]

Maritain himself realizes the obscurity of his exposition when he

[2]G. Vahanian, *op. cit.*, p. 96-7.
[3]Jacques Maritain, *True Humanism*, Charles Scribner's Sons, 1946, p. 103.

says that the Christian's activity in this world makes secular history
become, somehow, a preparation for the kingdom of God. How does
this come about? Maritain does not know. It is something "enig-
matic." Elsewhere he affirms that "the history of the Church is already the commencement of the Kingdom of God in its beginning
in time, while the history of the secular world will only come to its
ultimate end by means of a substantial 'mutation', described as the
conflagration or burning up of the world, by which it will be born
into the Kingdom."[4]

In this last passage Maritain clearly reveals his dualism. Secular history as such does not lead to the kingdom of God, but disappears
before it to let it pass by. There is a "substantial mutation." Profane
values do not seem to be integrated or saved in the eschatological
conclusion of the Kingdom of God; on the contrary, they are at best
substantially changed after a "worldly conflagration."

Maritain's thought will become more clear when he attempts to
define the "specific difference" between what he calls the *temporal
and spiritual* orders. Culture and civilization belong to the temporal
order, and are found there for a terrestrial purpose. Nevertheless at
the same time they must have reference to "that eternal life which
is the end of religion.[5] This "ennoblement of culture in its own
order"[6] realized by grace is not something intrinsically connected with
the temporal order but is only an invasion of the "spiritual" from
above into the earthly sphere in order "to procure the earthly good
fortune and the development of the various natural activities of man
in strict relation to his eternal interests and in a way which facilitates
his access to his supernatural end."[7]

According to this view culture becomes at most the stage on which
the totally transcendent divine embraces the human person.

The "spiritual" intrudes into the "temporal" to look for and rescue
the human person and prepare for his entrance into a totally different
order. "The order of faith and the gifts of grace, being concerned with
an eternal life which is a participation in the intimate life of God
himself, constitute an order to which the name *spiritual* must rightly
belong and which, as such, transcends the temporal sphere. And if

[4]J. Maritain, *op. cit.*, p. 94.
[5]J. Maritain, *op cit.*, p. 90.
[6]J. Maritain, *op. cit.*, p. 90.
[7]J. Maritain, *op. cit.*, p. 90.

for the Christian this spiritual order should vivify and elevate the temporal order, it is not because it is any part of the temporal order, but, on the contrary, because it transcends this and is absolutely free and independent of it."[8]

The action of the spiritual on the temporal is reduced to changing the world into the "field of a truly and fully human life, i.e., one which is assuredly full of defects, but it is also full of love, whose social forms are measured by justice, by the dignity of human personality, by brotherly love."[9]

As we see, the spiritual evaluates *per se* the moral dimension of the human person. All the other "profane" values are intrinsically alien to grace, and their subordination to the spiritual order besides being extrinsic implies in the long run a retreat and disappearance to wait for the moment of that "discontinuous" transition from the temporal to the eternal.

Maritain takes pains to distinguish his position from that of Karl Barth. For the latter, man has to deny himself totally before God. The divine or spiritual does not give value to any moral dimension of man. He is and remains intrinsically sinful and unjust. Besides, history does not prepare anything for the eschatological entrance into the kingdom. The latter takes place at an a-temporal point, in some sort of existential "now" above and beyond any chronological succession. For Maritain, on the contrary, the spiritual, starting right now, penetrates the human person and assumes and ennobles man's moral dimension, thus preparing him for access to the eschatalogical kingdom of God. "In the Barthian view, the history of the secular world can in no way prepaie a positive growth of the Kingdom of God, even enigmatically and on condition of that essential discontinuity which is marked by the final mutation and separates the 'next to the last' from the 'last.' "[10]

Perhaps Maritain's conception of the ultimate supernatural end of the person as practically coinciding with this discontinuous leap from history into the kingdom of God offers us the possibility of a better understanding of his thought on this issue.

"This Christian, indeed, is never *resigned*. His conception of the city holds in it of its very nature the wish to adjust the conditions of

[8]J. Maritain, *op. cit.*, p. 90–91.
[9]J. Maritain, *op. cit.*, p. 104.
[10]J. Maritain, *op. cit.*, p. 104, note 1.

this vale of tears so as to procure a relative but very real earthly happiness for the assembled multitude; a structure in which all can find a good and decent living, a state of justice, of amity and prosperity making possible for each the fulfillment of his destiny. He claims that the terrestrial city should be so directed as effectively to recognize the right of each of its members to live, to work and to grow in their life as persons. And the condemnation which he pronounces on modern civilization is indeed more grave and more reasoned than that of the socialist or the communist, since it is not only the terrestrial happiness of the community, it is also the life of the soul and the person's spiritual destiny that are menaced by this civilization."[11]

According to this way of thinking, the destiny of the human person is something rigidly pre-established and qualitatively identical for every man. The succession of generations only increases quantitatively the number of "saved" persons. It is possible to conceive an advance from the viewpoint of greater opportunities and greater possibilities offered man for growing to moral maturity in regard to the achievement of his "spiritual destiny" understood exclusively as the "life of the soul." The only thing that *intrinsically*—after being assumed and ennobled by grace—prepares the attainment of this spiritual destiny is the moral life that matures and fulfills itself in profane history. The extra-moral culture as such must be addressed by faith to ensure that this culture (1) does not hinder or impede the free development of the supernaturalized moral dimension, and (2) offers the *extrinsic* contribution of a favorable climate for such development.

The contribution of profane values, because it is extrinsic, bears the stamp of the provisional. These same profane values, in the day of the "worldly conflagration" when the human person is about to take that discontinuous leap toward the kingdom of God, will only be fuel to feed the fire of personal destiny of a spirit which in the kingdom will live free and relieved of all that "worldly" material which nourished it throughout history.

From this Maritainian viewpoint we can understand and evaluate the nucleus of his fundamental distinction between the two types of Christian civilization: medieval Christendom and the "new Christendom" which he himself proposes.

---

[11]J. Maritain, *op. cit.*, p. 131.

Medieval civilization was sacral. Essentially and basically it considered all the profane values—cultural, social, and political—as mere instruments for the realization, from that very moment, of the kingdom of God on earth. Its ideal was the Sacrum Imperium which was never fully realized in history, but which ruled the civilization of the time as a powerful myth. Naturally ecclesiastical authority de facto exercised a specific jurisdiction over all branches of human activities: scientific, philosophical, social, and political. The Church as such had her schools, hospitals, and prisons. In many cases the sacred ministry was intimately linked with strictly political functions and in any case the secular arm placed its sword at the service of the spiritual arm.

Maritain considers this sacral type of Christendom as outdated and proposes a profane type. The difference between "sacred" and "profane" is reduced to the binomial "instrumentality-autonomy." In both cases there is—there must be—a subordination of profane values to the supernatural mission of the Church. In sacral Christendom this subordination was understood in an instrumental sense, as if the secular city—human culture—renounced its own freedom and autonomy and put itself completely at the service of the sacred ministry, which would use it fully as instrument for the achievement of its own purposes, namely the progressive establishment, throughout history, of the kingdom of God. "In the case of a civilization of the secular type, it is in the pursuit of its own proper (infravalent) end and as the (subordinate) principal agent that the temporal city acquits this office with regard to the Church: then it is rather in integrating Christian activities in its own temporal work (e.g., in giving Christian instruction its just place in the scholastic curriculum, or in asking religious institutions of charity to take their rightful part in works of public assistance), and in so receiving itself, as an autonomous agent in free accord with an agent of a higher order, the aid of the Church, that the city will assist the latter in the fulfillment of its rightful mission."[12]

On the practical level the difference is reduced to the fact that cordial and benevolent dialogue takes the place of authoritarian and dogmatizing monologue. The Church will not command the Christian state to use force to eliminate heresy. Furthermore she will

---

[12]J. Maritain, op. cit., p. 173.

benevolently see to it that "this vitally Christian lay state"[13] "assures the heretic his liberties as a citizen, and accords him the juridical status appropriate to his ideals and his habits."[14]

Maritain thinks of medieval Christendom as a "ghetto" that attempted to enclose all profane values within its walls in order to use them—willing or not—in function of the only necessary thing: the kingdom of God.

For this reason he proposes that the walls of the Christian "ghetto" be torn down and that the Church become some sort of "Christian *diaspora*, a Christendom not grouped and united in the body of a homogeneous civilization, but spread over the whole surface of the globe like a network of centers of christian life disseminated among the nations."[15]

Frankly, Maritain's vision of the new Christendom appears heroic when we consider it in its ideological presuppositions, as we have done above. Maritain wants to maintain a purely sacral concept of humanism while avoiding by every possible means the consequences of "sacralization" of the temporal Christian regime.

Indeed, for Maritain the progressive development of profane culture (in its political dimension included) is not intrinsically related to the kingdom of God. The only thing that will be "saved" beyond the eschatological frontier is the moral spiritual dimension of the human person. All else will perish in the "conflagration of the world." Maritain does not explain the reason why profane history enjoys its own distinct existence. What is the nature of its progress? Why is chronological succession multiplied? Perhaps its only reason is that it permits the multiplication of "the human persons" who will achieve their spiritual destiny beyond this temporal order.

If profane history, then, does not have in itself any transcendental finality, why not accelerate the process of conflagration from the other side, i.e., of sacred history, effectively preparing the fuel to be burned in the great echatological fire? Why should the Church decide to stand idly by, letting history take its course, a history which is bound to disappear in the name of a kingdom of God that totally transcends it and from which it is separated by a gulf of discontinuity, a gulf across which a "substantial mutation" will take place?

In Maritain's humanism, human effort—work—lacks a sufficient

13J. Maritain, *op. cit.*, p. 175.
14J. Maritain, *op. cit.*, p. 174.
15J. Maritain, *op. cit.*, p. 249.

explanation. Why does humanity wearily ascend the painful hill of its own advancement on the basis of progress growing in all dimensions, and with inescapable implications in the cosmic context, in which it develops? Would it not be better to suppress that useless strain by an invasion which invades from above into the area of the profane in order to change it definitively into the only thing worth our while, that is, into a favorable area for the moral expansion of the baptized man?

We fail to understand how this profound conception of sacral humanism fails to arouse an irresistible drive among the most enthusiastic and militant elements of the Christian camp to renew on a large scale the great medieval experiment of the *Sacrum Imperium*.

Maritain's liberalism and tolerance are indeed a humble confession of failure. Deep down, nevertheless, they imply no abandonment of the attitude—decidedly erroneous—of the sacral Christendom of the Middle Ages.

Ernest Troeltch defines Christian influence on social ethics as a mere "compromise." It is in the long run, "a tremendous continuous compromise between the Utopian demands of the Kingdom of God and the permanent conditions of our actual human life."[16]

Actually, Christianity no longer has the opportunity to "be a tyrant" over the new culture by converting it into a pure instrument, which is what the medieval mythology attempted in fact to do, according to Maritain's description. For this reason it retreats and attempts to effect a compromise with the new civilization.

"But it would be a mistake," warns Vahanian, "to assume therefore that Maritain is attempting to reverse the age-old dogmatism and exclusivism of Christendom. It would be a mistake to think that this new version of a Christian culture distinguishes itself by its openness and an inherent attitude of tolerance toward heterogeneous elements. What Dr. Maritain's position clearly spells out is not the toleration of non-Christian elements. The converse is the case. Unconsciously, if not consciously, Maritain is presenting the fact that henceforth it is probably Christianity which will need the toleration of others."[17]

[16]E. Troeltch, *Christian Thought, Its History and Application*, Meridian Books, New York, 1957, p. 177.

[17]George Braziller, Inc.—from *The Death of God* by Gabriel Vahanian, reprinted with the permission of the publisher. Copyright © 1957, 1959, 1960, 1961 by Gabriel Vahanian.

Vahanian himself goes straight to the point when he warns that for a possible survival of Christianity as the inspiration of the new culture, there must be between them a direct and intrinsic relationship. As soon as this relationship is, as happens in Maritain's case, indirect and extrinsic, there is no alternative left but a mutual subordination. In the middle ages culture was subordinated to religion. Now in the "new Christendom," Maritain's ambition—though he may not admit it—is to subordinate religion to culture.

In brief, Maritainian humanism has not ceased being "sacral." Man's existential realization is intrinsically independent of the continuing movement of the great cosmic machinery in which he lives rather as a guest and pilgrim than as an integral part and complex member of this ongoing evolution. It is quite significant that Maritain scarcely refers to the eschatological resurrection. And when he does, he shows his radical misunderstanding of a theme that in the soteriology of the New Testament—especially in Paul—belongs to the essence of the faith.

"To my mind it is a betrayal at once of man and of God not to understand that history is a movement towards the Kingdom of God and not to wish for the coming of that Kingdom. But it is absurd to think that it will arrive *in and as a part of history*, where good and evil are inextricably intertwined. Prepared by the growth of history, and by the progressive mixing and refining of the human being that it involves, it will come *at the end* of history, at that hour of the resurrection of the dead to which all history leads."[18]

Maritain's metaphor is very revealing. History acts as a furnace in which man is refined and destined to a meta-historical life totally discontinuous from and unconnected with the upward movement of the cosmic context in which he developed. We fail to understand how Maritain imagines this human being, "mixed and refined" in the cosmic furnace, under a guise of resurrection.

Maritain's humanism cannot be taken as representative of genuine Christian thought. Basically it implies a dualism (world-God, history-kingdom) in flagrant contradiction of biblical anthropology and soteriology. Indeed if there were no resurrection "those who have fallen asleep in Christ, are lost." (1 Cor. 15:18) "If for this life only we have hope in Christ, we are more to be pitied than all other

[18]J. Maritain, op. cit., p. 52.

men." (1 Cor. 15:19) "Why am I in peril every hour? If from human motives, I fought wild beasts at Ephesus, what use was it to me? If the dead are not raised, 'Let us eat and drink, for tomorrow we die.' " (1 Cor. 15:30, 32)

Consequently, man's self-advancement, as demanded by biblical soteriology, includes intrinsically and directly all those human values that Maritain calls "profane." In his opinion, these profane values "only" operate extrinsically and indirectly to help create a "climate" favorable to the development of human personality, a personality inadequately conceived in its merely moral and "spiritual" (in the dichotomous sense of the word) dimension. In the biblical perspective these "profane" values have to be saved in their own historical and spatial context. Until they acquire adult maturity through an evolutionary process, they cannot be integrated into the Kingdom of God.

Grace is not reduced to making possible man's moral dimension. On the contrary, it penetrates every corner of his existential constitution. "Sacral" humanism seeks to confine the original invasion of the Kingdom of God to a single aspect of human and worldly evolution: the moral one. This aspect alone, duly transformed, will penetrate the frontiers of the Kingdom. For this reason, all the other manifestations of human culture are transient and provisional. In relation to the Kingdom they will have been able to act only as pedestal, a favorable climate, a removal of obstacles. But in the long run, they are not meant for salvation. They will perish without appeal in the final conflagration.

Such is the reason why the human effort—work—does not, in this humanistic vision acquire a sufficient justification, why it finds itself humiliated and degraded.

In biblical humanism, on the contrary, human effort is *intrinsically* necessary, although not *sufficient* to achieve the total and full development, the resurrection. As long as humanity has not reached a certain level of maturity it will not be ready for resurrection. Without the influence of grace human effort cannot reach its fulness. But grace is not to take the place of this effort. It only makes it possible, heals it in its roots, and ennobles it. This is why grace radically refuses any confinement to a "ghetto." Grace has to get lost among things, among efforts, among the stages of the progressive evolution of history. This also is the highest aspiration of Maritain for his "new Christendom." He envisions it as a "sort of Christian *diaspora*, a Christendom not grouped and united in the body of a homogeneous civilization, but spread over the whole surface of the globe."[19]

The intuitive spirit of the great Catholic philosopher has made him firmly accept this conclusion despite an intrinsic inconsistency with his dichotomous view of Christian man.

Hence it also follows that the ministry of grace must equally avoid any temptation to a "ghetto." The *Sacrum Imperium* is basically incompatible with this biblical concept of the intrinsic salvation of history. Grace does not provide the leadership and government in the upward march of humanity. Instead, it illumines and strengthens it.

The *Sacrum Imperium* as such tends to build up a "Christian city" within whose walls human life as a whole develops in a servile position of total subordination to the "sacred" and the "spiritual." The ultimate and deepest motive of this attitude is the low esteem of "profane" values, which are denied an intrinsic and direct relationship with salvation. Consequently the tendency is to tame them, to make them pure instrument of the one human dimension that, ennobled by grace, will enter the gates of the Kingdom of God in the eschatological outcome.

We have seen how this purely moralistic conception of man fails in its foundation. Biblical humanism is deeply interested in the whole human reality. This reality must be saved by a process of intra-historical maturing, anointed by grace—by a grace dispersed and lost among things.

Naturally the "ministry of grace" has to be organized rigidly to fulfill as effectively as possible this mission of self-dispersion among all ascending values of history. To do this it has to retreat, becoming a "church," an "assembly." But this "ecclesialization" is not an end in itself. It is a means to better achieve the end: "The anointing of all things." (St. Justin)

The *Sacrum Imperium* tended to convert the means into an end. It sought to rally the forces of the Church and turn her into a self-sufficient fortress perfectly walled in and well supplied with all needed resources.

European Christendom was an experiment, not fully successful,

[19]J. Maritain, *op. cit.*, p. 249.

according to Maritain, in putting into practice the medieval myth
of the *Sacrum Imperium*. Renaissance humanism meant a rebellion
of "profane values" which were unwilling to be considered as merely
outdated and provisional instruments for the attainment of full
human development. If Christianity refused to offer them the
prospect of intrinsic salvation, they would look elsewhere for a way
to overcome the multiple "alienations" which had left them subject
to the tyranny of other "lords" and harnessed to the aristocratic
chariot of a ruling minority.

The cry of liberation of Renaissance humanism was simply a deep
longing for the total salvation of all human values.

The *Sacrum Imperium* in its outrageous attempt, carried on with
every means at its disposal to enslave all "profane" values, constituted
a permanent temptation for the Church with respect to her essential
function of vigilance and prophetic denunciation. Like the prophets
of the Old Testament, the Church is the representative of divine
transcendence, and as such she has to infiltrate all historical manifestations, but without losing her identity. Her pre-eschatological
attitude is constantly *militant*, that is, involved in a struggle against
the human and angelic freedom which up to "the day of the harvest"
has a mysterious and divine license to follow a deviationist path.

She therefore has to accept the struggle, and logically, the presence
of the enemy. She cannot devote herself to annihilating him. She
has to allow for his physical expansion, to which he has a certain
divine right. Her activity has to be preferentially "testimonial"—
"martyrial"—deeply humble, and courageously insistent. She must
lead the way in passing a positive judgment of salvation on human
values, and she must offer this salvation in a humble and persuasive
manner.

In the *Sacrum Imperium*, the secular arm was at the service of
the ecclesiastical arm to obtain, at times by violence, the submission
of profane values. In the opening speech of the Council Pope John
XXIII pronounced the funeral oration on the Constantinian era of
the Church, an era which seems destined to disappear forever: "The
princes of this world, indeed, at times in all sincerity, intended thus
to protect the Church. But more frequently this occurred not without
spiritual damage and danger, since their interest in the matter was
guided by views of a selfish and perilous policy."

At the opening of the great council, the Church, through the

Pope, thanks all the agents of the *Sacrum Imperium* for the services rendered, but "prefers to use the medicine of mercy rather than that of severity. She considers that she meets the needs of the present day by demonstrating the validity of her teaching rather than by condemnation. She opens the fountain of her life-giving doctrine which allows men, enlightened by the light of Christ, to understand well what they really are."

As Christ did to his disciples at the last supper, so the Church has answered those who—undoubtedly in all sincerity—still offered her the two swords, "That's enough!" (Lk 22:38)

In brief, the "new Christendom" dreamed of by Maritain is dawning on the horizon of a new era, although the achievement of its future effectiveness will require it to sever the umbilical cord connecting it to the sacral and dichotomous conception of the *Sacrum Imperium*. The Church is seriously attempting her own purification and limiting herself to her truly prophetic function.

"Human values" have nothing to fear from the "new Christendom." The old message of Christ passes a positive, intrinsic, and effectively salvific judgment on them. This is the only type of salvation that fully corresponds to the exertion, accumulated through the centuries, of this tired Sisyphus, man.

CHAPTER 11

THE CHURCH AND HER RELIGIOUS FREEDOM

The problem of religious freedom which was in the spotlight at the most important discussions of Vatican Council II, runs the grave risk of being misinterpreted by observers outside the Catholic Church. At times one gets the impression that the Church, forced by external difficulties, is finally yielding some of the ground she holds in order to insure her survival in a situation she no longer controls. Perhaps this interpretation of the "new attitude" of the Church has arisen because of the lack of a purely theological presentation of the problem of religious freedom, leaving aside elements introduced from natural law or from the legal systems of the cultures in which Christianity historically developed.

In this chapter I will attempt to present the problem merely from the point of view of its biblical possibilities. As a basis, I will refer to Paul's doctrine—essential to this matter—supporting it with evidence from the rest of the New Testament.

The word "Freedom" in Paul

The first thing an honorable presentation of the problem demands is the elucidation of those texts which apparently could be introduced as the highest expression of Paul's doctrine on this problem of religious freedom which we now consider. We must here begin by recognizing that many pauline passages containing the word "freedom" or a related term have nothing to do with our modern preoccupation.

"Freedom" for Paul has three main meanings.

a.) *Social condition:* Society at Paul's time was divided, from the sociological point of view, into free men and slaves. (1 Cor 7:21–22; 12:13; Gal 3:28; Eph 6:8; Col 3:11) From the very outset of his preaching Paul proclaims the radical Christian opposition to this social discrimination. At the beginning the leveling would occur only in the ecclesial community, but logically this "religious" equality would inevitably spread to other realms of human life, as happened historically.

b.) *Possibility of personal option:* This sense of freedom was very common in popularized Stoicism, which undoubtedly is present in the Pauline expression. In practice it was identified with the *autopragia* or existential possibility of deciding for oneself. (1 Cor 7:38–39; Rom 7:2–7; 1 Cor 9:1)

c.) *Religious freedom:* Although the expression seems ambiguous, we cannot honestly leave unqualified this sense of freedom, very frequent in Pauline soteriology. For the Jew (and later for the Christian) religion is a "service" (*douleuein*) of the living God (1 Thes 1:9; Rom 12:11; 14:18; 16:18; Acts 20:19). Christians—especially the Apostle—are God's servants" or "Christ's servants" (Acts 2:8; 4:29; 16:17; Rom 1:1; Gal 1:10; Phil 1:1; Col 4:12). The theme of "religious freedom" is intimately connected with the theme of "service." The service of God becomes liberation from the ancient servitudes: sin, idolatry, and law. This is the theme that is developed at great length in chapter 5 of Galatians and in chapters 7 and 8 of Romans.

The famous phrase of Galatians, 5:1, "Christ has set us free to enjoy freedom" must be interpreted in this concrete context. In the preceding chapter Paul had described both conditions in great detail: the "slave" in the religious sense, is the man stripped of divine grace and left to his own forces, faced by a higher law showing him a goal of human fulfillment which he cannot reach by his own means. The "free man" is the man-in-Christ who has received grace and been endowed with the resources belonging to a "son" so as to be able to attain with them that existential fullness to which he so anxiously aspired. By "Freedom" Paul does not mean here the psychic faculty of choosing between contraries or contradictories, or least of all, the openness toward a juridical or moral sovereignty. For him, "freedom" is the condition of the "children of God," who being "children" possess the "spirit of God," (3:6) with which they are intrinsically enabled to overcome the great alienations: sin and death. For this reason he strongly encourages the believers to "remain" in that state of freedom. The coming of the Holy Spirit into men is conditioned by free human acceptance. It is not enough that at the beginning the Galatian community had received the Spirit. It has to continue to collaborate freely with God's activity, so that the Spirit may remain. The return to the proud position of the *kauchesis* necessarily involves a giving up of "freedom" (the condition of possession of the spirit) and a return to the previous condition of slavery: "Do not be caught again under the yoke of slavery."

As we see, Paul's treatment of the problem of "freedom" does not refer to the concrete modern question of "religious freedom."

From conscience to conscience

When we today face the problem of religious freedom, we are moving in an area divided up by the confluence of two human realities: individual conscience and social conscience. May an individual conscience—or the conscience of a more or less large group—convinced of the rightness of its position, allow a free hand to the development of other individual (or group) consciences that are considered to be in error? Or on the contrary, does the upright conscience have the right to use external means of repression to hinder the social manifestations of other consciences?

Thus presented, the problem finds a precise answer in the doctrine of Paul and in other texts of the New Testament. I am not concerned here with natural law. I am only interested in finding out if the Christian has a positive valid norm for adopting either of the two possible positions on this question.

Neither the Old Testament nor the Gospels contain the notion of moral "conscience," even though the reality expressed therein is not unknown. It appears in the New Testament only in Paul's writings. Ignored by Palestinian Judaism it was very common in the Greek world. From the axiom "everything belongs to the wise man" (*tou sofou panta einai*) Greek philosophy jumped to the idea of a privileged "right" (*exousia*), reserved to the wise man. The learned man was a man of upright or formed conscience, and it gave him the right to take over the control of the social family, even using political means of repression. It was enough to be right to begin to act and organize society with a hard hand.

Paul introduces an authentic novelty into this rigid formulation of the rights of the upright conscience. In the community of Corinth there was a group of Christians—"wise" or "gnostic"—who had a clear conscience with respect to the eating of meals previously sacrificed to the idols. Paul himself takes sides with them, assuming as objectively right their appraisal of conscience. Nevertheless, next to the "strong" or men of formed conscience were the "weak," those who, also in good faith, had not been able to overcome an imperfect state of conscience, and thought that it was sinful to eat food that had been offered to idols. Paul, against every Stoic tradition—to which he clearly refers—introduces the novelty of "religious freedom." The "strong" have to be considerate of the situation of those of erroneous conscience. I think it is interesting to give Paul's own text with its original force: "As for eating food offered to idols, we know well that an idol stands for no reality in the world, and that none is God save one. For although there may be so-called gods in heaven or on earth—as indeed there are many 'gods' and many 'lords'—yet for us there is but one God, the Father, from whom all things have their being who is our last end; and there is but one Lord, Jesus Christ, through whom all things have their being and through whom we are. But, not everyone has this knowledge. Some, by force of a habit still enduring, in regard to idols, eat food as really offered to an idol; and their conscience, being weak, is defiled. Yet it is not food that will place us near God. We lose nothing if we do not eat, and we gain nothing if we do eat. Only take care lest this liberty of yours should become a stumbling block to the weak. For if any one sees you, a man of knowledge, at table in an idol's temple, might he not be encouraged, if his conscience is weak, to eat food offered in idol worship? And so by your knowledge this weak man is destroyed, this brother for whom Christ died. Thus sinning against your brethren and wounding their conscience when it is weak, you sin against Christ. Therefore, if food is a cause of my brother's falling, I will never eat meat, lest I cause my brother to fall" (1 Cor 8:4–13).

"All things are permissible, but not all things are helpful. All things are permissible, but not all things build up character. Everyone should seek his neighbor's advantage rather than his own. Eat whatever is sold in the market without asking any questions for conscience's sake. For 'the earth is the Lord's and everything in it.' If any one of the unbelievers invites you to a meal and you wish to go, eat whatever is set before you without raising any question for conscience's sake. (But if some one says to you, 'This has been offered in sacrifice,' then out of consideration for the man who informed you, and for conscience's sake—I mean his conscionce, not yours—do not eat it). For why should my liberty be determined by another man's scruples? If I partake with thankfulness why am I denounced because of that for which I give thanks? So, whether you eat or drink, or do anything else, do all for God's glory. Give no offense to Jews or to Greeks or to the Church of God. Just as I try to please all men by seeking not my own advantage, but that of many, that many may be saved." (1 Cor 10:23-33)

Paul repeats a similar teaching to the Romans. (Rom 14:1-15:13)

Although here we have not yet reached the crux of the modern question of religious freedom—since Paul is dealing with the interaction between two different internal groups of the same ecclesial community—nonetheless precisely because of this, we can draw an argument *a fortiori*. If within the one community of believers who accept the spiritual authority of the leaders it is necessary to have this unbelievable respect for the erroneous conscience of a "brother", how can we not suppose that in a pluralistic society there must be an even greater obligation for absolute respect for the other conscience?

Final and eschatological character of God's judgment

Those texts in which Paul, following the whole apocalyptic tradition of the Old Testament and the direct preaching of Jesus, affirms the definitive and eschatological character of God's judgment, are decisive for a clear formulation of a Christian charter of religious freedom from a strictly theological point of view.

"With me it is a very small thing that I should be judged by you or by any human court. I do not even judge myself. True, my conscience makes no charge against me, yet I am not by that fact acquitted. My judge is the Lord. Therefore do not pronounce judgment before the time, before the Lord comes, who will bring to light the secrets now hidden in darkness and will disclose the intentions of men's hearts. Then every man will receive his due praise from God." (1 Cor 4:3-5)

The judgment, in the biblical sense of the word, is not merely the utterance of an opinion on the behavior of others, but an authentic exercise of an efficient authority which effects what it has determined. Let us remember that when they first settled in Palestine, the political leaders of the Jewish society assumed the name of "judges," that is, true authorities with effective executive power. Paul considers as sacrilegious the attempt to seize the right which only Christ will exercise at the end of history, "when he comes to judge the living and the dead." Meanwhile, there must be a coexistence of error and truth. To want to suppress by coercion the error, or the erroneous conscience, or its manifestations, is a sin of eschatological impatience: "Do not judge before the time. Wait for the coming of the Lord." The whole revelation of the New Testament finds its simplest and most illuminating expression in the parable of the wheat and the weeds. (Mt 13:23–30, 36–43) Here we have a very adequate framework for the problem we are facing. Christ himself affirms that "the field is the world." (Mt 13:38) Naturally Christ's disciples are interested directly in the conservation and propagation of what they consider "pure wheat." But they cannot make use of repressive means to make the weeds disappear. Both wheat and weeds have a mysterious safeconduct that will allow them to grow until "the harvest," which is explicitly identified with the "end of history." (Mt 13:39)We can speak in this sense of "the right of weeds" of positive divine origin. "Let both grow until the harvest." (Mt 13:30)

The Church, as People of God, has not received the mission to exercise this "efficacious judgment" during the period of eschatological ripening, in salvation history. Only at the end when Christ returns in the *parousia* "the saints will shine like the sun in the kingdom of their Father." (Mt 13:43) That is, as Paul explicitly mentions alluding to the same text of Daniel 12:2 and 7:22: "Do you not know that the saints are to judge the world?" (1 Cor 6:2)

Meanwhile the Church has to accept the "divine right" mysteriously possessed by the weeds of coexisting with all the manifestations of grace in the great era of the world. Christians, therefore, even if they were unable to deduce from natural law the need to respect the rights of an erroneous conscience, would be obliged to do so in virtue of an explicit instruction of positive divine origin.

Religious freedom in Church-State relations

The problem of religious freedom receives specific light from the New Testament considerations on Church-State relations.

Oscar Cullmann's thesis, according to which the state appears in the New Testament linked with the invisible powers (Paul's *exousiai*) seems to maintain its exegetical validity, despite the attacks to which it has been subjected.[1]

In order to fully understand this Church-State relationship, it is necessary to grasp the profound significance of *cosmos*, since the state authority is exercised within the cosmos and intimately and essentially belongs to it.

We leave aside the passages where cosmos has a merely spatial or temporal meaning without theological nuances. (Rom 1:20; 1 Cor 8:5; Gal 4:3; Phil 2:16; 1 Cor 14:10; etc.) We limit ourselves to the texts in which it is a definitely theological expression.

In the first place, cosmos means mankind, but considered as being in a pejorative condition of rebellion against God. The New Testament passes a theological judgment on this world. It is just the opposite of a *theosfera* or the totality of possibilities and conditions of life (1 Cor 3:22; 7:13 ff); the persons themselves in their attitudes and judgments (1 Cor 1:20, 27) or in a state of sinfulness and enmity with God. (Rom 3:6, 19; 11:15; 2 Cor 5:19) When the "world" is identified with this kind of *hamartios-fera* the New Testament uses the concrete expression "this world" corresponding to the rabbinical expression *òlam ha-zeh*. (Jn 8:23; 12:24, 31; 13:1; 16:11; 18:36; 1 Jn 4:17; 1 Cor 3:19; 5:10; 7:31)

The world, taken in this pejorative sense, is ruled by the powers of the devil: "the prince of this world" (Jn 12:31; 16:11; 1 Jn 5:19); "The god of this age" (2 Cor 4:4); "angels, principalities, powers" (Rom 8:38; 1 Cor 15:24); "the leaders of this age." (1 Cor 2:6-8); "the elements of the world." (Gal 4:3-9) These are the "enemies of God" who at the end will be annihilated by Christ. (1 Cor 15:24-26) The leader of all these anti-divine powers is Satan (Rom 16:20; 1 Cor 5:5; 7:5; 2 Cor 2:11; 11:14; 1 Thes 2:18); the "god of this age." (2 Cor 4:4)

The cause for this sinful dimension of the "world" is formally attributed to these "powers" as such, that is, insofar as they are the incarnation of "power." Hence the names of expressing power: "principalities" (1 Cor 15:24; Eph 1:21; 3:10; 6:12; Col 1:16; 2:10, (Eph 3:10; 6:12; Col 1:16; 2:10, 15). From this point of view

[1]O. Cullmann, *The Christology of the New Testament*, London, 1957; Bibliography in Clinton D. Morrison, *The Powers that Be*, London, 1960, p. 40.

the concept of "power" or "authority" (equivalent to "state")
appears in the New Testament as one of the realms of the devil.

Lk 4:5–7: The devil affirms that to him "all authority (exousia)
has been given, and its splendor, and he can give it whom he
wills." He is the great emperor of the world, appointing the chiefs
of State as his lieutenants.

1 Cor 2:8: "This world's rulers (archontes)" did not know
"God's designs" and for this reason they "crucified the Lord to whom
belongs all glory." Here there is a clear reference to the State
15; Tit 3:1), "powers" (1 Cor 15:24; Eph 1:21; 1 Pet 3:22; Cfr.
Rom 8:38), "dominations" (Eph 1:21; Col 1:16), "wordly leaders,"
authorities that de facto decreed Christ's crucifixion, namely Herod
and Pilate (Lk 23:12; Acts 4:27; 13:27). Now then, these "rulers"
are clearly identified with the "powers of the devil." The same
things are said of both: (1) They are "destined for destruction"
(katargoumenon, 1 Cor 2:6; katargese pasan archen kai pasan
exousian kai dynamin); (2) they did not know God's designs (1 Cor
2:8; Eph 3:10).

This theme of identification between the "state powers" and the
"powers of the devil" is developed in the characteristic style of
the Apocalypse. The "beast" has "seven heads, which are seven
kings" (17:10) and "ten horns, that are ten kings." (17:12)

However this "power of the devil" which is so often incarnated
in the earthly counterpart of the civil or State power is not an
absolute force that can oppose God on an equal level as the Gnostic
and Manichean dualism maintained. On the contrary, the "powers"
are part of God's plan centered in Christ. These "powers" were
created in Christ, through him and for him (Col 2:16). Even
as they were successful in the Lord's apparent failure at his crucifixion (1 Cor 2:8) they were radically beaten in his resurrection
(Col 2:15), but not totally destroyed, since the Christians still
have to struggle with them (Eph 6:12 ff). They will, however,
be destroyed by Christ at the end. (1 Cor 15:24 ff)

Nowadays these "powers" are still going strong, but since the
resurrection of Christ they are harnessed to his triumphal chariot
(Eph 2:15) and cannot carry out their designs. To put this in a
demythologizing formula, "the powers" are still one of the greatest
sanctuaries of human selfishness and pride. They have, nevertheless,
a mission to accomplish within the design of divine wisdom as
revealed in Christ.

From this perspective we can now understand Paul's exhortation to the Romans to "submit to the ruling authorities." (*exousiais*, 13:1) True, Paul affirms that "there exists no authority not ordered by God. And that which exists has been constituted by God, and therefore he who opposes such authorities resists the ordinance of God." (13:1-2) But in his mind, as is obvious from the rest of his writings (and even in Romans), the concept of State authority as such does not come into the picture as a positive ideal in the progressive construction of the Kingdom of God.

The "Lordship" of Christ will be fully realized only after history has ceased. Today the Church is the only place where this "Lordship" is exercised. The "lords" that embody State power throughout history have no intrinsic relationship with the "Lordship" of Christ. They have only an extrinsic and subordinate one. Despite their strong "diabolic" tendency they can and must serve God's design. And for this reason the State authority is called by Paul "servant of God for men's good," "bearer of the sword," "servant of God to execute his wrath on the wrong-doer," "ministers of God attending to the taxes." (13:4-6)

But he never hints, even remotely, that the "State authorities" have a direct and active participation in the progressive proclamation and establishment of the Kingdom of God in the evolution of history. The "powers," and their temporal embodiment, the State, have been made subject to Christ, and are even used for extrinsic purposes, such as the exercise of civil power as described by Paul in Romans, chapter 13.

It follows that the situation of the Church in regard to the State is based on a dialectic tension of submission-independence. On the one hand, the Church does not claim to replace the State in public services ("bear the sword, attend to taxes, execute the wrath") but on the contrary, totally yields to its regulating power even "for the sake of conscience." (Rom 13:5) But on the other hand, she is jealous of the salvific mission which Christ entrusted to her as a monopoly. The *Kerygma* is proclaimed only in the realm of the Church and with a specific mission which goes back to Christ himself. The "powers" receive from the Church the proclamation of the mystery of God. (Eph 3:10) This "soteriological" independence of the Church with regard to the State demands that the Church always and necessarily maintain a critical position *vis-à-vis* the "power of the State." The "state" is still a

place of diabolical attraction. The "powers" try from time to time
to shake off the yoke of Christ's Lordship. This is manifest in
the attempts of the State to declare itself and act as "absolute
Lord." The formula of primitive Christianity *Kyrios Iesous Christos*
must be understood as a firm, strong reply to the absolute and
deifying pretensions of the State power, which are concretized in
the other formula *Kyrios Kaisar* which undoubtedly exceeded the
limits of "servant of God, minister of God, bearer of the sword,
etc." aiming at a totalitarian absolutism with religious overtones.[2]

To sum up, Church-State relations are to be regulated by the
basic principles of this dialectical tension: submission-independence.
The State cannot take over the ecclesial area of Lordship of Christ
by assuming a kerygmatic or soteriological duty which belongs to
the Church exclusively. And the Church must never contest the
State's function of regulating society for the common good. This
equilibrium is upset when either one goes beyond its function,
trespassing into the other's realm, and specifically:

a) when the State thinks it is the ultimate degree of human
possibilities and assumes absolute uncontrollable power. This excess
can also be in the disguise of "Christian State". In this case the
State has taken over the ecclesial function, gagging the Church in a
paternalistic manner in the name of a supposedly evangelizing contribution;

b) when the Church is internally organized in the pattern of
a civil society and becomes a more or less powerful rival of the
latter. The intrusion of "temporal power" into ecclesiastical persons
and functions goes directly counter to that "submission to authority"
Paul speaks of in Romans, chapter 13. When this tension has
been broken on either side the Church loses the great gift of
"religious freedom" which is part of her nature, as willed by Christ.

Against an absolutist State the Church must defend her "religious
freedom," that is, the freedom to proclaim publicly the "lordship"
of Christ. This "Lordship" of Christ implies a transcendent exclusive-
ness: there is but one Lord, and every one else is a "servant of
Christ." (Col 3:22–4.1; Eph 6:5–9) Therefore, the Church cannot
remain silent in the face of the frequent attempts of the different
"lords" who endeavor from their position of power to create and

[2]W. Forster, *Hern ist Jesus*, 1924, p. 106, and O. Cullmann's reply, *op. cit.*,
p. 172, note 1, and p. 190.

maintain any kind of human discrimination. The kerygma of the Church must cry out against the concentration of human goods or values in the hands of a few, since this is actually an attempt on the uniqueness of the "Lordship" of Christ. In this case the supposedly political neutrality of the Christian community when faced with a "lord-like" power is treason against the core of her creed: "Jesus Christ is the Lord."[3]

The ecclesial Kerygma is not kept in the clouds of a comfortable angelism, but must crash-land wherever there is an idolatry of power, that is, a usurpation of the unique Lordship of Christ

But in order to fulfill this mission of prophetic denunciation against a "lord-like" usurpation on the part of the State, the Church herself must remain spotless and clean; that is, she must avoid contamination with "civil society" by keeping herself to the religious realm where the unique Lordship of Christ is proclaimed. A Church bound up with the State—through the concession of social privileges, educational monopolies, or sociological representations—powerfully limits her "religious freedom," her capacity for prophetic denunciation. In this sense, it can be understood that reduction of the Church to strictly religious dimensions, far from relieving her of her unavoidable human task, makes her capable of fulfilling her mission as salt of the earth and light of the world. "Civil" contamination weakens the ecclesial salt and dims the light of the Gospel.

In brief, a proper relationship of Church-State, according to the New Testament, is a necessary condition for the achievement of the great ecclesial good of religious freedom. Non-Christian religious groups should not fear that their freedom would be curtailed by a supposedly "Christian" State, since according to the New Testament point of view we have just analyzed, the State must not become contaminated with the Church or vice versa. "My kingdom is not of this world. If my Kingdom were from this world, my subjects would fight that I might not be surrendered to the Jews. But my kingdom is not of this world." (Jn 18:36)

The Church jealously guards her exclusive right to proclaim the Lordship of Christ and does not humiliate herself by entrusting to the State the custody and protection of her own religious reality.

---

[3] O. Cullmann, *op. cit.*, p. 169.

In this sense, a Church-State relationship, in virtue of which the State commits itself to bring its "power apparatus" to the service of the Church, would go against the New Testament concept of religious freedom. The Church "not being of this world" does not accept military or political alliances with the "powers" of *this world*. She carries her religious freedom of prophetic denunciation all the way to the painful consequences of martyrdom.

Conclusion: "Religious freedom" is a supreme good pertaining to the innermost being of the Church. It is above the temporal exigencies of any historical circumstance.

The Church has received from Christ the mission:

a) to respect and even protect the subjective erroneous conscience of the neighbor, though without prejudice to her mission to preach the gospel;

b) "not to pull out the weeds" before the last day of the eschatological judgment, and to give up any coercive means of destroying the enemy and the dissenter;

c) to remain pure within her own domain as a religious community, which is the only place for the proclamation of the "Lordship" of Christ, avoiding contamination by "civil society" and adopting a respectful and critical position with regard to the State without demanding from the latter the use of its power apparatus to protect the proclamation of the Gospel which will always move in different channels from those of the designs of the temporal power. (1 Cor 1:20)

The right of admission and exclusion within the Church

Our viewpoint would not be complete if we did not add something which at first may seem to contradict what we are saying: the right of the Church to admit believers into her midst or to dismiss them from the ecclesial community. Paul himself frequently exercises this right at times in a negative sense (1 Cor 5:1–13). However, even in the case of the excommunication of the incestuous person at Corinth, Paul warns that the measures adopted are valid only in the ecclesial domain and from a purely religious point of view. They can in no way be applied to the profane level of social coexistence.

"I wrote in my letter not to mingle with fornicators. I did not at all mean this world's fornicators, or the greedy and robbers, or idolaters. In that case you would have to withdraw from the world. But rather I wrote to you not to associate with any one who bears the name of brother if he is a fornicator, or is covetous, or an idolater, reviler, drunkard, or robber—not even to eat with such a one. For what business is it of mine to judge outsiders? Is it not those within the fold whom you are to judge? God judges those outside. Drive out the wicked person from your midst." (1 Cor 5:9–13)

As we see, the Church is recognized as having the right of any normal society to set limits and conditions to those who attempt to join her. But outside her own confines she cannot exercise an executive power that obviously does not pertain to her.

Nevertheless, even the exercise of this executive power of admission or dismissal of her own members has to be exercised by the Church in a deeply constructive climate.

At the beginning of the same second letter to the Corinthians, Paul proclaims this sense of deep understanding that he is going to exercise through his apostolic authority: "Not that we lord it over your faith, but rather we work with you for your happiness." (2 Cor 1:24)

Here Paul is using a concept often found in his writings, especially in his correspondence with Corinth: the apostle is a humble "servant," a mere "minister of Christ," not a tyrant over the community of believers. (2 Cor 4:5) It is far from Paul, then, to come to the Church as a *kyrios*, seizing the unique and exclusive function of Jesus. The same idea is found in 1 Cor 3:5. The parallel with 1 Cor 1:24 is impressive. If Paul is a mere "minister through whom faith has come," logically he cannot become the "ruler of their faith."

Hence, we are not concerned here with the power of "controlling the faith" which the apostle would refuse for himself (since it is precisely in 1 Corinthians that "he defines" authoritatively several dogmatic questions), but with the "humble" position that Jesus himself demanded from the rulers of the Church (Mt 20:27; Mk 10:41, 45; Lk 22:24–30; Jn 13:13). As we can see in the texts given, such a position does not suppress or deny the full authority of those in command, but only prevents the proud and tyrannical abuse of that authority.

For Paul the exercise of apostolic authority is humble cooperation with the stimulus to "joy" that makes a community grow and advance in Christ, for he is tired after the hard struggle in Ephesus: "We do not want you to be ignorant, brothers, of the affliction which befell us in Asia. We were crushed beyond measure, beyond our strength, so that we despaired of life itself. Why, we felt that we had received the sentence of death. The purpose of that sentence was to bring us to rely not on ourselves but on God who raises the dead. He it is who delivered us from so deadly a peril, and he will deliver us. And in him I have put my hope that he will deliver me again. You also must help me by prayer, so that many will give thanks on our behalf for the blessing granted us in answer to many prayers." (2 Cor 1:8–11) Paul does not appear as the invulnerable ecclesiastical ruler who, in order to avoid contamination, teaches, exhorts, argues, condemns, and absolves from a lofty platform. For him authority is not being a *servant* but it is also being a *beggar.* He comes before the faithful extending his hand to beg human warmth and affection.

"I made up my mind not to make you another painful visit. For if I cause you pain, who is there to gladden me but the one whom I have pained? And I wrote as I did, that when I came I may not be pained by those who ought to give me joy. For I felt sure of all of you, that my joy would be the joy of you all. For I wrote you out of much affliction and anguish of heart and with many tears, not to cause you pain but to let you know the overflowing love I have for you. If any one has caused pain, he has caused it not to me, but in some measure—not to put it too severely—to you all. For such a one this punishment meted out by the many is enough. So now you should rather turn to forgive and comfort him, or he may be overwhelmed by too much sorrow. For this reason I exhort you to reaffirm your love for him. For this is why I wrote, that I might test you and know whether you are obedient in everything. Any one whom you forgive, I also forgive. What I have forgiven, if I have forgiven anything, has been for your sake in the person of Christ, to keep Satan from gaining the advantage for we are not ignorant of his designs." (2 Cor 2:1–11)

This "apostolic document" of Paul is a marvelous model of how authority must be exercised in the Church in a climate of authentic "religious freedom." The ecclesial leader is not ashamed to show openly his most human traits. He does not impose a priori his authority, but modestly "begs" the community of believers to grant forgiveness to the condemned. Furthermore, that same forgiveness granted by Paul is conditional pending the communal decision of the church.

The second letter to the Corinthians ends with an impressive exhortation by Paul in which he clearly acknowledges his own apostolic authority and invites the ecclesial community to revise and readjust their behavior: "Examine yourselves, to see whether you are living up to the faith. Test yourselves. Do you not recognize that Jesus Christ is in you?—unless indeed you fail to meet the test! I hope you will find out that we have not failed. And we pray God that you may do no evil—not that we may appear to have met the test, but that you may do what is good, and we may not be incapable of passing the test. We can do nothing against the truth, but only for the truth. And so we are glad when we are weak but you are strong. What we pray for you is improvement. I write this while I am away from you, that when I come I may not have to be severe in my use of the authority which the Lord has given me for building up and not for tearing down." (2 Cor 13:5–10)

According to this pauline text ecclesiastical authority should be exercised within the following existential circumstances:

(1) There should be an examination of oneself in an atmosphere of communal responsibility: "Examine yourselves, to see whether you are holding to your faith."

(2) There should be a primacy of the objective good of the believers even at the price of possible loss of prestige to the ruler of the community: "Not that we may appear to have met the test, but that you may do what is good and we may not be incapable of passing the test."

(3) Authority must be exercised in subordination to the superior norm of an objective truth: "We cannot do anything against the truth, but only for the truth."

(4) The purpose for the exercise of authority must only be a constructive one: ". . . I may not have to be severe in my use of the authority which the Lord has given me for building up and not for tearing down."

(5) And above all, the disciplinary procedure of *katartisis* (2 Cor

13:9) must be employed: the "rehabilitation" of the condemned, both internal—psychological and spiritual—and communal, trying to smooth and make comfortable this joyful readmission to the community of believers.

Conclusion: These observations are simply an attempt to provide a starting point in the touchy and important problem of "religious freedom." A purely biblical perspective cannot resolve the whole problem, since it is sociologically conditioned by many historical and human factors, which go far beyond the restrictive framework in which the word of God was incarnated.

But we can at least begin with a careful reading of the Bible since fidelity to a positive word of God and not the mere external pressure of present circumstances must dictate our attitude.

As we have just seen, we find in the Bible definite indications of a positive will of God that makes us adopt an attitude of coexistence. We are authorized to find support only in the power of the Spirit so that we can humbly and gently offer the service of an authentic proclamation of the gospel to the world.

CHAPTER 12

THE CHURCH AND ATHEISM

In the Pastoral Constitution on the Church in the Modern World we have been given what is probably a more complete treatise on atheism than any ever before written, even in an academic theological work. I will limit myself to outlining the themes of the Council document, stressing a few points and making some comments.

Humanistic atheism, as a mass phenomenon, is modern

The first assertion of the conciliar constitution is the sincere acknowledgment of a new fact on a mass scale in present day society: ". . . growing numbers of people are abandoning religion in practice. Unlike former days, the denial of God or of religion, or the abandonment of them are no longer unusual and individual occurrences."[1]

This massive incidence of atheism is not simply a denial of God in general, but a very concrete form which we could call "humanistic atheism." Indeed the negation of God or of religion "is presented (this is not rare today) as requirements of scientific progress or of a certain new humanism."[2]

We can accordingly see why the builders of the new society are moved to institutionalize this atheism as a necessary condition for their task of construction. "In numerous places these views are voiced not only in the teachings of philosophers, but on every

[1]Pastoral Constitution on the Church in the Modern World, no. 7, op. cit., p. 445.
[2]Ibid., p. 445.

side they influence literature, the arts, the interpretation of the humanities and of history, and civil laws themselves."[3]

The specter of humanist atheism loomed large over the Church gathered in council, as Paul VI so well put it in his closing message: "Secular and profane humanism has appeared, in all its impressive stature, and in a way has threatened the Council."[4]

Consequently the first attitude of post-conciliar catholicism must be that of a full awareness of a fact of massive proportions which envelops us in its magnitude, and which cannot be taken lightly.

The Vatican document, with great phenomenological sensitivity, refers almost exclusively to this humanistic atheism leaving aside all other forms of historical atheism still found in our society, such as the scientific, sociological, and even religious atheism. Religious atheism is found especially in one of the most widespread forms of buddhism, called Hinayana ("small vehicle").

Humanistic atheism is found concretely in the historical realization of marxism in our days. The description given in the Constitution refers precisely—though without naming it—to this historical fact which so greatly dominates contemporary reality. Indeed, as already mentioned, it was Karl Marx who was, if not the originator, at least the main agent in the diffusion of this critique of religion as "human alienation."

Marx adopts from Feuerbach not only the concept but also the expression religious alienation. According to Feuerbach, religion is the alienation of human essence in an unreal subject— God—upon whom man projects his own qualities. Marx accepts this thesis of anthropomorphic projection as the generating mechanism of the idea of God. But later he investigates the causes that set this mechanism in motion. Using Spinoza's and Hegel's suggestion, he attempts to explain the faith of the believer by his inability to make life meaningful. The absurdity of the real world impels man to seek refuge in God. But he criticizes those before him, especially Hegel, and their presentation of the problem of religious alienation on an abstract and idealist level, since the roots of religious alienation must be found in the economic and social disorder of society.

This is the sense in which Marx defines religion as being the

3*Ibid.*, p. 445.
4Closing message of Paul VI.

"opium of the people" insofar as it encourages man to avoid the task of human disalienation, offering instead an illusory compensation. The religion of the transcendent "externalizes all human relationships—national, natural, ethical—and dissolves the human world into a world of atomized and mutually hostile individuals."[5]

Christian morality especially, Marx continues, is like a "mystical cloud" watching over the social aspects of man's relations with other men and with nature. Man postpones his social realization and projects it forward to a transcendent world, concerning himself only with the task of perfecting himself as an individual so that he will have access to the social dream of an afterlife.

The issue is consequently "humanistic" atheism. God—the divine, the religious—is shown as a rival to man's creative autonomy, and consequently as an obstacle to true human progress. Man is actually committed more than ever to the Promethean adventure of his own realization on a cosmic scale, only to discover that the concept and profession of transcendence enervate and hinder this Promethean flight of the contemporary human enterprise.

This is not the time to describe, even briefly, all the manifestations through which this profession of humanistic atheism has come since the time of Marx and Engels up to the present day, including the political manifestations of socialism. The truth, however, forces us to recognize that it has come a long way from its beginnings in the powerful State organizations of a decidedly militant atheism up to the sincere and cordial dialogue that is being initiated before our eyes. R. Garaudy thus summarizes the critique which marxist humanism makes of the position of "the best Christians" in the dialogue: "We neither despise nor criticize the Christian for his faith, his love, his dreams, his hopes. Our task is to labor and to struggle, lest they remain eternally distant or illusory. Our task as Communists is to draw near to man in his most glorious dreams and his most sublime hopes, to draw near to him in a real and practical way, so that Christians themselves might find here on our earth a beginning of their heaven."[6]

As we shall see when we analyze the Vatican document, we must realize that on the Catholic side we have also come a long way.

[5]K. Marx, *A World without Jews*, Philosophical Library, New York, 1959, p. 43.
[6]R. Garaudy, *op. cit.*, p. 86.

Having left behind a mystique of hopes purely spiritualistic and of the after life, we have found anew the original concept of an eschatology totally present and committed to the historical reality of a humanity that moves under its own absolute responsibility.

Summing it up we can say that if historical marxism is getting farther and farther away from its primitive form of militant atheism, Catholicism is also getting rid of the old counterpart attitude of militant anti-marxism. And both now begin to meet on a common ground which is not yet satisfactorily defined for both parties, but which, without fear of error, I would define as a *common struggle against religious alienation*. From a purely phenomenological point of view, believers and unbelievers can face the same human reality and subject it to a purely scientific analysis. If this analysis shows that such a phenomenon—social, cultural, political, or religious—is alienating, both will honestly agree to join in the struggle for its removal from the upward route of human adventure. In this way, the anti-atheistic and anti-marxist militancy that formerly ferociously divided these two groups and kept them apart, is now beginning to become a single strong common militancy against the common enemy of this common human condition.

The eclipse of God

From this point of view the Council faced the massive consequences of the phenomenon that can be called the eclipse of God in contemporary society.

The constitution opens its discussion of atheism with this essential Christian assertion: "From the very circumstance of his origin, man is already invited to converse with God. For man would not exist were he not created by God's love and constantly preserved by it."[7]

God is not a part of human and cosmic reality. God does not appear to human consideration as an object of pure reflection. The Christian God is not the philosophical God demanded by the very structure of created being. He is the God of Abraham, Isaac, and Jacob. For this reason, the only way for God to make himself available to man is through dialogue. And it is God who is always open to dialogue.

7Op. cit., p. 456.

But the most fundamental point of Christian theology is the consideration of God's gratuity. Classical theology has formulated this basic truth in a traditional thesis: "Man was conceived and created by God in the supernatural order." The expression "supernatural," despite its theological precision, is subject to ambiguity for modern man. I consequently prefer to use again the biblical expression and concept of "gratuitous" God. The word "grace" and its derivatives pervade, as we know, the whole of biblical theology. And with it go the great theological words "gift," "love," "divine initiative," and "will of God."

If we could establish a hierarchy among the great Christian heresies that have risen in the last two thousand years, I would say that the most anti-Christian heresy, the one that most directly hurt the deep reality of God's presence in man and the world, was Pelagianism. Other heresies leave Christianity in bad shape, but it can still limp through history. Pelagianism pierces the very heart of Christian theology. It is the heresy that denies "grace," without thereby denying God. It is an attempt to handle God directly and make him a fundamental part of the human machinery.

One of the most subtle and profound forms of Pelagianism is the endeavor to include God as one of the elements demanded most profoundly by philosophy and science. The conciliar constitution condemns this attempt by simply presenting the opposite procedure as the only valid one by which to come into dialogue with God. "[Man] cannot live fully according to truth unless he freely acknowledges that love and devotes himself to his Creator."[8] Here we have a description of "faith" taken in a true sense such as shown in the Bible. Christians have committed a sin of sorcery in allowing this harmful modern form of Pelagianism to take over.

The Constitution recognizes that a great part of the guilt for this eclipse of God in the present world is a result of the opaque attitude of Christian thought and *praxis*. "Believers themselves frequently bear some responsibility for this situation. For, taken as a whole, atheism is not a spontaneous development but stems from a variety of causes, including a critical reaction against religious beliefs, and in some places against the Christian religion in particular. Hence believers can have more than a little to do with

[8]*Ibid.*, p. 456.

the birth of atheism. To the extent that they neglect their own training in the faith, or teach erroneous doctrine, or are deficient in their religious, moral or social life, they must be said to conceal rather than reveal the authentic face of God and religion."[9]

In brief, the attitude of scientific, philosophic, social, economic, and political sufficiency of many Christians has been the cause that "the genuine face of God has been concealed." A Church, blinded and heavy with the burden of the undue luxury of pseudo-knowledge and of power not her own, has lost the transparency necessary to make present to man the face of a purely gratuitous God. Christians, as such, have committed the sacrilegious act of using our God magically as an expedient to resolve all sorts of problems. We have attempted to make grace a bothersome rival of nature. The Church, as an institutionalized ministry of grace, has judged herself powerful enough to absorb within her walls all the possibilities of human evolution and has often assumed undue control of history, claiming a supposedly divine mission for that purpose.

Fortunately today, in Vatican Council II the Church humbly acknowledges her position as a disciple of truth and of the objective reality of the human condition. "[The Church] gratefully understands that in her community life no less than in her individual sons, she receives a variety of helps from men of every rank and condition. For whoever promotes the human community at the family level, culturally, in its economic, social, and political dimensions, both nationally and internationally, such a one, according to God's design, is contributing greatly to the Church community as well, to the extent that she depends on things outside herself."[10]

Therefore a struggle against atheism cannot be conceived in the form of threatening condemnations, but in the form of sincere revision of the attitude of "Christendom" still strong in our midst. The fact that the Church and her institutions are intimately connected with the social and political reality of the human community hinders or keeps her from "free acknowledgment of the love of God," the only possibility, according to the Council, of entering into dialogue with God. In our old Christian societies there was an authentic "religious inflation" that made it possible

[9]*Ibid.*, p. 457.
[10]*Ibid.*, n. 44, *op. cit.*, p. 491.

for men to adhere to religion, not by a purely religious choice, but by a more or less gentle sociological construction.

A re-evangelization of our society demands from us primarily the task of dismantling with all haste the secular apparatus of a Church which had assumed control of the buttons and levers of human knowledge and activity.

Confessional atheism

This modern form of Pelagianism was largely responsible for the birth of the kind of "confessional atheism" described so accurately in the Vatican document. "Modern atheism often takes on a systematic expression which, in addition to other causes, stretches the desire for human independence to such a point that it poses difficulties against any kind of dependence on God. Those who profess atheism of this sort maintain that it gives man freedom to be an end unto himself, the sole artisan and creator of his own history. They claim that this freedom cannot be reconciled with the affirmation of a Lord who is author and purpose of all things, or at least that this freedom makes such an affirmation altogether superfluous."[11] The last sentence of this conciliar text summarizes a position that I would define as "atheistic deconfessionalization." The "affirmation" that there is a God "is altogether superfluous."

Recently a French atheist, Roger Ikor, has described this "atheistic deconfessionalization." "I do not mean to say that science proves that God does not exist. What I say is that science has expelled God from the universe. God who at the beginning was our only teacher and the great ruler of the world, no longer contributes anything to our knowledge or to its functioning. He does not act on the causes, primary or secondary, or on the consequences, immediate or mediate. He exists, if he exists at all, elsewhere, in a different manner, but certainly not as the creator of the universe or—and this is more serious—not even of man. At least, we can without him explain everything that is real. I do not doubt at all that this new impulse of science, apparently crucial, is a crisis for the believer."[12]

[11]*Ibid.*, n. 20, p. 458.
[12]R. Ikor, *Dieu aujourd'hui*, Paris, 1965, p. 63 ff.

Here we have a new point of agreement between believers and unbelievers. Corresponding to the atheistic confessionalism that used to believe that the absence of God really explained the mechanism of human evolution, there was on the Christian side a deistic confessionalism that made God a fundamental, although immanent, piece of the great cosmic machinery. Historically God and the religious "gnosis" had been misused to explain the enigmas of human knowledge or to fill up the *lacunae* of our ignorance. But as man discovers the immediate causes of that cosmic reality in which he lives, the "deist" influence of that falsely immanentized God was also retreating. There were times when the Bible was considered the absolute encyclopedia of all human knowledge. Little by little philosophy and science forced the Bible to retreat, pushing it into its purely religious domain. In the origin of modern atheism a prominent spot is occupied by the struggle—today inconceivable to us—against the insistent affirmation of the great Galileo ". . . *eppur si muove.*"

The conciliar constitution basically refers to the confessional position of atheism: the assumption that the expulsion of God is by itself an explanation of human reality.

On the other hand, following the Vatican Council directive, we Catholics must also renounce deist conformism, and in a certain sense we can answer Roger Ikor that this new drive of science creates no crisis for us. Our God, the living God of Abraham, Isaac, and Jacob, has never been presented in the Bible as the immanent solution to cosmic and human reality. He has always been a big question mark hanging over our lives that has never been resolved into a concrete and exhaustive answer.

Attitude of the Church

We do not mean by all this that the Church should not assume a strong and firm attitude against the phenomenon of modern atheism. On the contrary, the Constitution tells us, "in her loyal devotion to God and men, the Church has already repudiated and cannot cease repudiating, sorrowfully but as firmly as possible, those poisonous doctrines and actions which contradict reason and the common experience of humanity, and dethrone man from his native excellence."[13]

[13]*Op. cit.,* p. 458.

A dialogue, cordial as it may be, demands from both sides a sincere and clear affirmation of their positions, excluding as dishonest any form of courteous or tactical reticence. For this reason, the Catholic Church strongly opposes the phenomenon of atheism. However, her attitude is full of understanding and humility and can be reduced to the following outline:

(A) In the first place the Church carefully examines the phenomenon of atheism, studying as objectively as possible the historical causes that have produced it. [The Church, however,] strives to detect in the atheistic mind the hidden causes for the denial of God; conscious of how weighty are the questions which atheism raises, and motivated by love for all men, she believes these questions ought to be examined seriously and more profoundly."[14]

With this the Council rejects the superficiality of so many pompous condemnations uttered out of fatuous ignorance by false preachers, who prefer to proclaim the God of bourgeois deism rather than the true God who has given us his final word in Christ.

It has been affirmed all too lightly that it is inconceivable that an atheist could be in good faith. The Vatican document does not lend support to this harsh and harmful judgment since it admits that there are deep and serious reasons that have made the present situation of the atheist possible.

(B) In the second place, the Council admits that the motives given by humanistic atheism do not weaken the religious reality of Christianity. These motives can be reduced fundamentally to two: (1) religion is a bothersome rival of human autonomy; (2) the eschatological hope is an obstacle for the authentic progress of men.

(1) With regards to the first reason—the harm to human autonomy—says the Council document: "The Church holds that the recognition of God is in no way hostile to man's dignity, since this dignity is rooted and perfected in God. For man was made an intelligent and free member of society by the God who created him, but even more important, he is called as a son to commune with God and share in his happiness."[15] A careful reading of the biblical cosmogony shows that this latest affirmation of the Church is connected with the old position of the first books of the Bible.

For the Semites—let us recall—"to name something" was equiva-

[14]*Ibid.*, p. 459.
[15]*Ibid.*, p. 459.

lent to having a transforming power over that reality. In the
Genesis creation account God names those things that first condition man: heaven, earth, sea, sun, day, night. But he leaves the
animals nameless. When on the sixth day he creates man, he
immediately brings to his presence the birds of the sky and the
animals of the earth "to see what he would call them, and whatever man called every living creature, that was its name." (Gen 2:19)
The biblical God finishes his work and begins his sabbatical leave,
transferring the creative initiative to the hands of man, without
interfering with the autonomy of his continuing creation. As we
have seen, biblical man sins against God when he wants to escape
his task of worldly construction, just the opposite of Prometheus
in Greek cosmogony who sins against the gods in attempting to
steal the fire of technology and arts. There is an open date for
Prometheus in the Christian calendar.

(2) The second argument adduced by humanistic atheism against
Christian religion is the presumed obstacle caused by its eschatological hope. The Vatican document is very explicit in this regard:
"[The Church] further teaches that a hope related to the end of
time does not diminish the importance of intervening duties but
rather undergirds the acquittal of them with fresh incentives."[16]

Those of us who have worked for years with great hopes on the
preparation of a "theology of the world," have seen with satis-
faction that our modest theological efforts have been taken into
consideration by the Council document in incorporating this eschatological vision into its text as something meaningful (both immanent and transcendent) with regard to the creative effort of human
history. In this regard I prefer to speak, not of an "eschatological"
sense, but rather an "eschatologizing" sense in human evolution.
The presence of the kingdom of God in the world is eschatologizing it, impressing on it the rhythm of the second coming which
will lead it to the final stage of the divine design for the world:
the leap to the kingdom of God. The late Cardinal Albert Meyer,
picking up this biblical view, began the discussion in the Council
of the draft Constitution on the Church in the World Today, and
it is easy to see the imprint of his interpretation in the following
paragraph: "The expectation of a new earth must not weaken

[16]*Ibid.*, p. 459.

but rather stimulate our concern for cultivating this one. For here grows the body of a new human family, a body which even now is able to give some kind of foreshadowing of the new age.

"Hence, while earthly progress must be carefully distinguished from the growth of Christ's kingdom, to the extent that the former can contribute to the better ordering of human society, it is of vital concern to the kingdom of God.

"For after we have obeyed the Lord, and in his Spirit nurtured on earth the values of human dignity, brotherhood and freedom, and indeed all the good fruits of our nature and enterprise, we will find them again, but freed of stain, burnished and transfigured, when Christ hands over to the Father: 'a kingdom eternal and universal; a kingdom of truth and life, of holiness and grace, of justice, love and peace.' On this earth that kingdom is already present in mystery. When the Lord returns, it will be brought into full flower."[17]

With this return to an authentic biblical eschatology—all of it occupied with the success of the material universe in which man lives—the Church cleans up the residues of that evasive mystique of *contempt of the world* which, despite its undeniable values, has contributed to the reality of the modern humanistic atheism we are now considering.

(C) Finally, the Constitution points out some concrete objectives for reaching a human and positive contact with the reality of the phenomenon of atheism.

(1) The first objective is an "adequate exposition of the doctrine." A deep revision of our Christian theology is urgent. As we have seen, the two polarities of this theological revision are reduced, on the one hand, to the gratuitous and absolutely transcendent character of God and religion and, on the other hand, to the acknowledgment and appreciation of human values in their autonomy and personality.

A theology of the world must be built up in which this dialectical tension between the two polarities of transcendence and incarnation is not broken. A theology of the transcendent at the expense of the incarnation leads to an attitude of disdain for and obliviousness of the every day reality of the human task. And a theology of the incarnation without due attention to transcendence leads to positions akin to "christendom": the Church falls into the temptation of

[17]*Ibid.*, p. 480.

mistaking the kingdom of God with human evolution and logically demands for herself the baton in the great orchestra of life.

And since, according to the dictum that "extremes meet," it frequently happens that from the polarity of transcendence one jumps to the polarity of incarnation, through a hypocritical dichotomous attitude. Thus we find again with great frequency the case of the austere and secluded monk who from the solitude of the monastery goes abruptly to rule with strong hand the destinies of a nation.

(2) A second area of revision with regards to atheism deals with the vital attitude of the Church: "The remedy which must be applied to atheism, however, is to be sought in a proper presentation of the Church's teaching as well as in the integral life of the Church and her members. For it is the function of the Church, led by the Holy Spirit who renews and purifies her ceaselessly, to make God the Father and his incarnate Son present and in a sense visible. This result is achieved chiefly by the witness of a living and mature faith, one trained to see difficulties clearly and to master them. Many martyrs have given luminous witness to this faith and continue to do so. This faith needs to prove its fruitfulness by penetrating the believer's entire life, including its worldly dimensions, and by activating him toward justice and love, especially regarding the needy. What does the most to reveal God's presence, however, is the brotherly charity of the faithful who are united in spirit as they work together for the faith of the Gospel and who prove themselves a sign of unity."[18]

This is a theme that has been amply developed in the Constitution on the Church: "God gathered together as one all those who in faith look upon Jesus as the author of salvation and the source of unity and peace, and has established them as the Church, that for each and all it may be the visible sacrament of this saving unity. . . . The Church is destined to extend to all regions of the earth and so enters into the history of mankind."[19]

The Church has the specific task of making God evident in the human family. For this reason she is the "sacrament of the world." A sacrament is a visible and easily intelligible sign. But God is not manifest except through the neighbor. Therefore the Church must

[18]*Ibid.*, p. 459.
[19]*Ibid.*, p. 84.

be a sign of this "neighborly" reality of humanity, as we have just seen in the Constitution on the Church in the Modern World: "What does the most to reveal God's presence, however, is the brotherly charity of the faithful who are united in spirit as they work together for the faith of the Gospel and who prove themselves a sign of unity." We should rigorously apply this criterion to all our Christian groups that pretend to be "churches." It is necessary that the people should easily be able to read this sacramental sign of unity and brotherly love in the reality of the Church. If on the contrary, the ecclesial mechanism appears to those outside as a rigid society folded in upon itself where powerful leaders oppress the faithful with declamatory threats, where selfishness in individual relations and ferocious rivalry among different groups abound, and in whose interior there is no air of evangelical freedom, then this so-called community of believers has dimmed its own sacramental reality, losing its own transparency and causing a real eclipse of God.

(3) Finally, the Constitution comes down to the concrete level of the daily common life of believers and unbelievers: "While rejecting atheism, root and branch, the Church sincerely professes that all men, believers and unbelievers alike, ought to work for the rightful betterment of this world in which all alike live."[20]

This cooperation must be preceded by a dialogue: "Such an ideal cannot be realized however, apart from a sincere and prudent dialogue." Today for a Catholic, dialogue is no longer a matter of choice, but strictly of obligation. One of the greatest sins we can commit is that of rejecting or avoiding contact with unbelievers. As we have seen, the conciliar Constitution refers to those who profess humanistic atheism, who ordinarily are marxists. Therefore, we Catholics are reminded officially of the grave obligation we have of speaking, living together, dialoguing, and acting together with our Marxist brethren.

Certainly this dialogue must be "prudent," but at the same time "sincere." A dialogue is not simply a handshake prompted by a weak feeling of hypocritical courtesy. Dialogue requires intellectual depth, sincere manifestation of one's own opinions, clear and complete exposition of the ideas, and above all a receptive attitude toward the other person. About dialogue the great Sevillian Antonio Machado used to say:

[20]*Ibid.*, p. 460.

"To dialogue,
ask first.
Then listen."

But dialogue is not merely an elegant form of intellectual fencing. It is above all and first of all, "cooperation." The Church professes that all men, "believers and unbelievers alike are to work for the rightful betterment of this world in which all alike live." Naturally this cooperation encompasses all the areas of human common life, but especially the social, economic, and political ones.

The first thing required by this dialogue and cooperation is the real and personal presence of the dialoguers. Many times we hypocritically establish a dialogue with Marxists, setting up some people from our own group as dummy Marxists. This is similar to a funeral in which the religious rites are celebrated over an empty casket, covered with a black cloth, without a corpse.

Recently in a dialogue with some Marxist friends in the amicable atmosphere of Rome at the time of the Council, we attempted to define and reject the anti-Marxist attitude of many Catholics. By anti-marxism I mean the position of those who affirm that the Marxist ideology and its holders can have no positive values whatsoever, that, if they do, another ideology must be made up and other forces must be gathered that incorporate into their program of action the minimal values "kidnapped" by the Marxists. The first position is a clearly Manichean one and totally opposed to the creational optimism of the Christian. The second one is a problem of "inflation of grace," that is, of believing that grace—and the ministry of grace, the Church—has to produce ex *nihilo* her own jurisdiction, creating all human values from scratch, competing thereby with all other human institutions and groups. And to show my Marxist friends that my viewpoint was radically Christian I quoted this impressive text from Luke: "And John answered, 'Master, we saw a man casting out demons in your name, and we forbade him, because he does not follow with us.' But Jesus said to him, 'Do not forbid him; for he that is not against you is for you.' " (Lk 9:49–50).

Naturally it is not easy to relinquish the nice cozy atmosphere of our old—and certain glorious—ecclesial "ghetto," to walk through the field and join the universal human team that attempts with great effort and high hopes to build up a better and more just world. But a strict command of our Christian faith and of our fidelity to the Catholic Church which so clearly exhorts us in her Council documents obliges us to undertake the painful effort.

Vatican Council II has got rid of painful riddles and has given us the humble and courageous impulse of Christian faith so that we may undertake the great human adventure without fear or reticence.

Only with the help of such a sincere and risk-laden commitment on the part of a Church which humbly extends itself to the whole human family will the eclipse of God come to an end for this old and glorious human race to which we Christians belong to the depth of our very being.